I0168072

Prompted, Prodded, Published:

How Writing Prompts Can Help All Writers

Debra R. Sanchez

Copyright © 2017 by Debra R. Sanchez

All rights reserved. This book or any portion thereof may not be reproduced, performed or used in any manner whatsoever without the express written permission of the publisher or author except for the use of brief quotations in a book review.

The anthology section of this book contains works of fiction, unless otherwise indicated. Names, characters, businesses, places, events and incidents in the stories are either the products of the authors' imagination or used in a fictitious manner. Any resemblance to actual persons, living or dead, or actual events is purely coincidental.

Printed in the United States of America

First Printing 2017

ISBN 13: 978-0692869758

ISBN10: 0692869751

Tree Shadow Press
www.treeshadowpress.com

For reproduction permission, contact:
Debra R. Sanchez
dbrsanchez@gmail.com

Cover art by Debra R. Sanchez.
Author photo by Melissa Schneider.

DEDICATION

To my family and my writing network,
thank you for your support and encouragement.
You let me be me.

In memory of Dolores (Deebella) Clark
You left too soon.

CONTENTS

PART ONE

PART TWO

ACKNOWLEDGMENTS

A special thank you to all who made this book possible.

To Laura, Linda, and Vicki from the Tuesday
writing group for helping create the prompts.

To the members of Write Club, Run of the Mills Writers,
Delmont Night Writers, Writers at Work, Writers in the
Dale, participants of Writing Success conference, and my
granddaughter Isabella, for writing and entering stories
and poems for consideration.

To my special panel of anonymous judges:
C, D, J, L, L, M from various towns in Pennsylvania,
E and K from Maryland, and A from Wisconsin.
Your help was vital to the selection process.

To all of the writers in the anthology section.
Without your words, this book would not exist.

To my family and friends who believed in me and put up
with months of endless prattle about the project.

To my writing mentors, James Perkins and Andrew Ade
for your continued support and encouragement years
after leaving your classrooms.

And, of course, to you, the reader. Whether you bought
the book to learn more about prompts or for the stories.

This book is for you.

ABOUT THIS BOOK

I am a firm believer in the power of prompts. I've led several writing groups over the years and found that one of the best ways to encourage the members to keep writing is to give them prompts. I find ideas for them in many places, and included some in the "Where to Find Prompts" chapter.

I'm always looking for new ways to keep my writing groups engaged and interested. Learn about how different types of groups work in the Groups section of the "Who Needs Prompts?" chapter.

My critique groups usually last about two hours. We start with members distributing copies of their writing to the others in the group. After reading and making comments on the pages, we discuss each piece. Sometimes everyone has something to share, occasionally no one brings anything. It's usually somewhere in between. On slow days I always have a writing activity to make good use of the time. On one such day, I invited one of my groups to come up with a set of prompts. Between us we came up with thirty.

Writers in different writing groups were given the list of 30 prompts and challenged to write a story for each. The list was also shared at a writing conference and online. No one completed the challenge. However, several managed to write more than one piece.

The next challenge was to choose the entries that would be included. Since the point of the book is to show how writing prompts can benefit writers at every stage of their writing career, it was important to choose pieces that represented all levels and ages of writers. To meet this goal, many wonderful stories went unselected.

There are stories by absolute beginners and by professional writers. The youngest writer was nine when she wrote her story for this book and the oldest has been retired for quite a while.

The writers had to use the prompts, but they had complete freedom to follow their imagination, even if it meant not exactly following the "rules" for the prompt.

HOW TO USE THIS BOOK

Prompted, Prodded, Published is divided into two parts.

The first section is a writing book about prompts: who needs them, what they are, when they are most beneficial, where to find them, why they are necessary, and how to use them. It also includes a chapter of prompts to exercise your writing skills.

The second section is an anthology of examples of how different writers used the thirty prompts. Each chapter begins with the prompt and an introduction followed by the stories.

Window

Susanna Fussenegger

(181 words)

My library has a meeting room with a great window. It covers an entire wall and has a handsome arch. Light streams in even on the darkest days. When the sky is blue and the clouds are fluffy, this window pretends we are outside.

"We" means me and my fellow dreamers. We play word chess once a week in the room. Words fly around in that bright light almost like soap bubbles at the children's fair. Oval and round tiny and giant they rise, they float, they glitter in the colors of the rainbow painting pretty chains of sentences that thrill. Other times, they just pop and die.

The window is watching. It knows that one-day the word chess players will come up with something so sensational that the word chains will shatter the glass and the glittery bubbles will fly up, up to the sky. They will push apart the fluffy clouds and with the skill of graceful ballerinas in colorful frocks, the bubbles will spell out the message:

"B E S T S E L L E R"

PART ONE

CHAPTER ONE

WHO NEEDS PROMPTS?

If you are a writer, you need prompts. All writers use prompts. It's a fact. Every story, poem, essay, play, or anything else ever written is a product of a prompt.

Before you scoff at this idea, consider the definitions of the word "prompt" from the following sources.

Merriam Webster Dictionary:

Transitive verb
1: to move to action: INCITE
2: to assist (one acting or reciting) by suggesting or saying the next words of something forgotten or imperfectly learned: CUE
3: to serve as the inciting cause of: evidence prompting an investigation

Noun
Something that prompts

Definition of Prompt for English Language Learners
1: to cause someone to do something
2: to be the cause of something.
3: to say something that encourages a person to talk.

https://www.merriam-webster.com/dictionary/prompt

Dictionary.com:

Verb
To move or induce to action
To occasion or incite, inspire
To assist by suggesting something to be said
Theater: to supply from offstage with a missed cue or line

Noun
The act of prompting
Something serving to suggest or remind

http://www.dictionary.com/browse/prompt

From these definitions, it is clear that for a writer the key ideas are that a prompt is something that will:

- suggest or inspire an idea to write about.
- move or induce you to write.
- encourage you to continue.

NOTE: These definitions do not say that a prompt must be imposed upon the writer.

Most of the time the writer will be inspired by a thought or idea that grows internally. Some writers are overwhelmed by a continuous onslaught of ideas that demand to be written. This is the very best kind of prompt. It requires little effort on the part of the writer except for deciding which idea to work on first.

This book deals with external prompts. Every writer will need such a prompt at some point in their writing career.

Beginners

Novice writers know that they want to write but may not know what they want to write about. This type is often given an assignment in a class and finds that they enjoy writing. They want to write more but may want or need more ideas to motivate them.

Prompts are an excellent tool for beginners. They can use the prompts to develop their writing skill. By using this book they can learn how to find prompts as well as how to create their own.

Experienced Writers

Writers with years of experience find themselves at a point where they have trouble coming up with new ideas. Some feel burned out. This is can lead to "writer's block" and is something that can be overcome.

Using prompts is an excellent way to break the block. This book provides insight to ways that prompts can help you to grow through these times. Ideas can also help you to hone your craft and develop new talents you may not know that you have.

Professionals

This type of writer uses prompts on a regular basis. They are frequently called assignments. It is not unusual for a professional writer to want to write something different in their free time. Something not assigned. Something not required.

However, they are often so used to writing things they are told to write that they may have a hard time coming up with ideas on their own.

Seasoned professionals can benefit from prompts in the same way that beginners and other experienced writers can. By using the suggestions in this book they may enhance their professional writing while exercising their skills for personal satisfaction.

Writing Groups

Individuals are not the only ones who use and thrive on prompts. Many writing groups depend heavily on prompts.

What Are Writing Groups?

A writing group is, as the name indicates, a group of writers. It can be thought of as: writing alone while writing together.

There are many types of writing groups. Each works in a unique way to provide support to its members.

Kinds of Writing Groups

- Critique Groups
- Assignment Groups
- Lecture Groups
- Online Groups

Each variety of group can benefit from prompts.

Critique Groups

Writers share their works in progress with the group. Depending on the size of the group and the length of the meeting there may not always enough time to review everyone's work. Likewise, it is possible that there may be times when none, or too few, of the members have something to share. The extra time can be used for writing exercises which are created from prompts.

Assignment Groups

The group is given a specific assignment/prompt and then shares what they wrote at the following meeting.

Lecture Groups

This is basically a writing class. The instructor talks to the class, either as a lecture or discussion, then provides an assignment. It may be for credit, as in a college class or for personal enrichment, as is typical with memoir or poetry workshops.

Online Groups

There are many writing support groups on social media sites and message board sites. They can use prompts to promote a writing exercise. Members frequently share information about contests or places looking for submissions. A great number of contests and markets either use specific prompts or have guidelines which instruct the writer to write in a determined manner, which can also be considered as a prompt.

CHAPTER TWO

WHAT ARE PROMPTS?
WHAT DO WE DO WITH THEM?

Writing prompts, as defined in the previous chapter, are basically ideas that trigger or direct any piece of writing.

When mandated by assignments or specific market or contest guidelines, they can be considered as rules. It is important to know when to follow the rules to the letter and when you can use them in a looser manner or disregard them completely.

For example, some assignments and/or contests require that a list of certain words be used. In this case you must follow the rule and include those words. It is often possible and desirable to use these words in unexpected ways. Writers who do so frequently do well in such contests.

Some submission requirements dictate the use of certain scenarios, characters, or actions. They may permit a loose interpretation of the given mandates, or they may insist on strict adherence to the specifics.

If your goal is to do well in such a contest, it is vital to read the rules and follow them. If you are writing an assignment for a graded class, it is in your best interest to follow the instructions in order to receive a good grade.

However, if you are using the guidelines for another reason, such as jump starting a project for your own purposes, it is perfectly acceptable and desirable to bend, twist, and even break the rules and guidelines to fit your needs.

The second part of this book is an anthology of short stories and poems that are the result of a contest. Thirty prompts were provided to several groups of people. The decision to include or exclude the pieces was made in part by how closely the writer followed the guidelines of each prompt. It was important that the selections were written by writers with a variety of writing skill. The one constant criteria that the judges were instructed to use was that the writer followed the prompt. For the most part, all of the stories and poems could be connected to the prompt that the writer chose to use.

There was one story that stood out for the way it neglected an important part of the given prompt. It is included in the anthology, however, as an example of how a writer can use a prompt without strictly adhering to the so-called rules.

Prompt #12 "A Sci-fi Story for Children, Hello Kitty Meets the Joker"

This was the most challenging and least popular prompt of the thirty. Only one person submitted a story. Although it was a science fiction story about Hello Kitty meeting the Joker, and there was a child in the story, it was not necessarily a story for children. The prompt was then sent to a group of children and one of their stories was selected.

The story that was not technically a children's story is included in the anthology as an example of using a prompt as a springboard to a storyline, even if some parts of the prompt are disregarded.

Bending, twisting, and breaking the rules can lead to wonderful things. If it isn't for a grade or strict contest, be daring and treat a prompt as a potential love interest. Be gentle. Don't force it to be something it isn't meant to be. But if it reveals itself to you and it leads you down a path you weren't expecting, enjoy the ride. Satisfaction is waiting for the audacious writer who takes a chance.

CHAPTER THREE

WHEN IS IT GOOD TO USE PROMPTS?

Writer's Block

Writers frequently are the victims of writer's block. This malady has plagued every writer from the dawn of the craft. This may occur due to fatigue or from over thinking your story or topic.

When writer's block happens, look for a prompt to keep your skills honed and ready to go back to your original work in progress. Using your writing time to craft pieces that are sparked from prompts is not a waste of time, although it may seem that way if you measure "success" by progress of your main project. Believing that you should only be working on what you are "supposed to" be working on can be harmful to your talents.

Do not fall victim to this way of thinking. Many fantastic stories will never be read because their authors hit a block and gave up. Countless promising careers never came to fruition due to lack of persistence and the inability to understand that taking a break to work on other projects isn't giving up. It is important to permit oneself the opportunity to do something different.

Try some of the following exercises to get through bouts of writer's block. It can be helpful to try them even if you don't have writer's block. Writing exercises can be as beneficial to the soul as physical exercise can be for the body.

EXERCISES – To Break Writers' Block

If you usually write:

- in a certain genre, try something new. Poets, try short stories. Sci-fi writers, try poetry.
- in a certain style, attempt to learn a new one. Non-fiction writers, try poetry. Playwrights, try filling in the details by writing a novel.
- alone in an office, try writing in a public place such as a coffee shop or library. Sometimes a change of scenery can get "the ink" flowing again.

Jump Start New Ideas

The most obvious time to use prompts is when you are unable to come up with an idea of your own. Using prompts as a way to launch a new story or other project may lead you in new unexpected directions.

Countless writers over the years have discovered an ability to create stories, poetry, plays, songs, and other projects by using a prompt. The unexpected becomes reality.

Explore the possibilities that surround you. Seek out opportunities to use prompts in ways that may do more than expand your catalog of works. Some can reward the wallet.

There are limitless possibilities to profit from prompts. Contests are an excellent example. Article writing is another. Keep in mind that it takes a lot of skill and practice to land paying writing gigs and perseverance to win contests. Don't let the difficulty deter you. Enter contests. Apply for writing opportunities.

The art of putting words together requires training and practice in order to be profitable. Practice will not make your writing perfect, but it certainly will make it better.

Avoid Burn Out

It is important to take a break and change things up a bit from time to time. It helps keep your writing fresh. By flexing your words in different directions, they become stronger. Such a practice can only enhance your writing and improve your ability.

Beyond looking for prompts, it is vital for a writer to read stories and other works that have been written from prompts. Many contests will post the winning pieces online. If you examine the prompt and the successful words, you can gain insight into what sort of writing can result in triumph. Study the style, but don't lose your own voice. You can emulate others while staying true to yourself. That is advice that no one should ignore.

Some websites can be used for exercising your craft by sharing your replies to a variety of challenges.

Mix Things Up

Try something new. The best way to develop a skill is to build on it. Learning to use different forms of writing provides an excellent method of developing new ways of thinking about all writing.

If you usually write long things, aim for something short, and vice versa. Here are some good options to try:

- Flash Fiction (under 500 – 1000 words)
- Greeting Cards
- Memoir
- Novella
- Plays
- Poetry
- Recipes
- Short Stories
- Songs

It is equally important to undertake different genres to flex your writing forces.

Below are some of the main genre forms. Many can be combined to create sub-genres.

- Articles (for magazines or newspapers, etc.)
- Children's
- Drama
- Erotica
- Fiction
- Fantasy
- Historical Fiction
- Horror
- Letters to the Editor
- Murder (or other) Mysteries
- Non-fiction
- Romance
- Realistic Fiction
- Science Fiction
- Speculative Fiction
- Spiritual
- Suspense
- Western
- Young Adult

Undoubtedly, there is something you have not tried. Pick one, or several. You may find that you have a flair and passion for multiple writing forms.

Personal confession: While writing this book, I hit a block that lasted for several months. Thanks to prompts, I wrote all sorts of things, poetry, memoir, short stories, newsletters, and some freelance work. I also wrote the notes for a workshop that I was asked to teach. But I avoided these chapters like the plague. I used prompts as a way to work through the block. I know they work. I believe in the power of the prompt. ~DRS, ed.

CHAPTER FOUR

WHERE CAN WE FIND PROMPTS?

Prompts are everywhere.

This is not an exaggeration. Everything you see, smell, taste, hear, touch or feel has the potential to be a prompt. You only need to release your imagination and find the endless possibilities.

Everyday Life

Keep a notebook, camera, or other means of recording the ordinary and extraordinary you experience. There are numerous apps available for smart phones for recording notes and thoughts using text or voice. Below is a short list of possible sources.

- snippets of overheard conversations
- remarkable happenings in the sky
- near misses whether while commuting or observing life
- antics of coworkers, friends, strangers, children, family, and pets
- anything that you experience that strikes you as memorable

The things you record do not have to be pleasant. Your writing does not have to be "nice and sweet" to be good. It certainly can be, but it is not required to be.

Books & Magazines

If you would prefer to use already created prompts, there are many books of varying quality to find ideas and story starters.

Many writing magazines offer prompts for their readers. An excellent source for this sort of prompt is available at writersdigest.com where they have contests and forums where people can share the stories and other writing they produce from these prompts.

Internet

The Internet is a never-ending source of pre-made prompts. Writing contests often require certain words, phrases, or situations to be included in the potential stories and poems.

If you use social media sites, there are a multitude of groups that are used as a means of getting the word out about calls for submissions. If you type "calls for submissions" in a social media search bar or your favorite Internet search site, you will find more sites than you can imagine. You can use "where to find," "call," or "submissions" as variations to broaden the results.

Anthologies

Anthologies, like this one, or the well known *Chicken Soup for the Soul*® series, usually include only pieces that meet certain criteria that is mandated by topic. The stories in this book are all the result of pieces written by people who entered a contest.

Contests

Some contests end in publication, others in monetary gain. Be sure to read the fine print and rules and conditions of any contest you enter. Sometimes the entity running the contest will own all future rights to your entry. Other times they only request first rights.

You can find contests the same way as suggested previously by searching for them with the search engine of your choice. Good key words include "writing contests" and your preferred genre.

Unusual News Stories

Did you ever see or read a news story that left you wondering how such an event or situation could have occurred? Did it make you want to know more?

Sometimes the actual reasons or causes of the story are so incredulous that they are omitted. Other times they may be tedious and ordinary.

The truth does not matter.

Yes. The truth does not matter. A writer can take the parts of weird or unusual news story and use them to create any fictitious story. Remember to change names and obvious details in order to avoid a potential lawsuit, but a writer can create whatever back-story or future outcome they want to from any source they choose.

Fantastical Family Lore

Do your relatives repeat the same tales every time they gather? Use those well-worn stories to weave a tapestry of family history.

It is practically impossible to properly capture the details of every conversation, but it is possible to imagine who said what and what the reactions and outcomes were based on the much repeated facts. This is sometimes called memoir or creative nonfiction.

Some examples that I have used, or may use someday include:

- mispronouncing a word in Spanish that caused an embarrassing moment.
- finding myself accidentally in a street riot, complete with tear gas, with my young son.
- losing a pregnancy.

- being locked out of my house.
- my father losing his dentures in the ocean.
- the time the dog ate my father's hearing aid.
- my grandparents being secretly married for months before anyone knew.

The possibilities and results can be humorous, scary, or heartbreaking. Life is full of stories and reasons to write them. Recording family history is vital to maintain a connection with future generations. If you want to do this kind of writing, the prompts are as close as a memory or conversation with a family member.

EXERCISES – Creating Your Own Prompts:

1.   Carefully observe your current surroundings. Make a note of three different things that you notice for each of your five senses.

2.   Take a picture of a common sight in an unusual angle.

3.   Listen to silence. What do you hear? (Hint: actual silence is practically non-existent.)

4.   Think of a moment from each year (or decade) of your life. What senses brought you the memory? Was it a voice? A smell? The sensation of heat or cold?

5.   Find an online magazine or other source for a prompt. Follow the directions.

6.   Using the same source and prompt, write something that bends or breaks "the rules" of the prompt.

7.   Check local newspapers or online news sources for unusual or weird headlines. Select one and write something about what the headline suggests to you. You do not have to read or use the story connected to the headline.

CHAPTER FIVE

WHY DO WE LIKE PROMPTS?

I surveyed members of several regional and online writing groups about prompts. This survey demonstrates that prompts offer similar and different experiences. Some writers may greatly enjoy a certain type of prompt while others dislike it. Like everything else in life, there is no one way to feel about prompts, and no one way to approach them.

Here are the questions followed by some of the answers.

(Note: Some of the answers were identical and were not included to avoid unnecessary repetition. Not all respondents answered all questions. Only the first and last sets of questions are cited to contributor.)

Question 1: What do you like about using prompts?

- They inspire thought, ways to play with theme and approach. It is interesting. A prompt can be approached a number of ways, depending on where the writer's mind labors at the time of use. I have published shorts inspired by prompts. ~ *Kerry E.B.B.*

- I like that prompts force me to write something I'm not typically comfortable with. It's like stretching or working a muscle. The exercise makes me stronger and gives me confidence to take bigger risks. ~ *Belinda C.*

- If I accept a prompt I feel accountable to use it, so it gets me writing when otherwise I may not due to time constraints. ~ *Esther D.*

- They give me something to write about. They make me write about topics I would not think of myself. One thing I have learned from prompted writing – one must research almost everything one writes about. ~ *Louise E.*

- I love seeing what other people come up with (in a group). It's amazing how different stories from the same prompt can be. ~ *Breana E.*

- They are stimulating. ~ *Susanna F.*

- Sometimes they cause sparks which lead to creativity. At times a prompt can spark an idea or story that had not occurred to you before. ~ *Vicki G.*

- Stimulates my mind to think creatively. ~ *John H.*

- I think that prompts can be the perfect cure for writer's block. They can focus your mind on a specific idea, line of dialogue, character, or setting and help get you writing again. ~ *Dana K.*

- I like when they're general enough that I can then use the assignment for sending to real life places (publications/projects). ~ *Laura L.L.*

- They give me ideas to write about for other stories, poems, books, etc. ~ *Jenifer M.*

- They ignite new thoughts in my brain. Immediately I start to think of ways I can create a short story out of the prompt. Many times the prompt is something I have not thought of before. When I finish my creation, I am pleased and surprised at my output. ~ *Christine M.*

- That some of the hard work has been done already: that is coming up with an idea. ~ *Megan V.*

- Good for self-discipline & just exercising one's writing chops. I think they are particularly good for people who are not actively working on something. ~ *Ruth W.*

Question 2: Is there anything you don't like about using prompts?

- I'm not a fan of the "take these 10 words and use them in a story" kind of prompt.

- They are not my ideas.

- Sometimes the topic does not interest me. it could be about a time in history I know nothing about.

- I don't like prompts that are too narrow.

- Sometimes there are no sparks and that makes me feel inadequate. At times a prompt can be like a giant roadblock to your creativity. Nothing about it inspires you. It always surprises me that I had NO idea of what to write while the person next to me comes up with a strong story.

- Sometimes they can be too restrictive. Ex: Story must use... Becomes restrictive & narrows the story.

- Sometimes I feel like they can be too specific and can force the story in a certain direction.

- I don't like ones that are so quirky or specific that I can't use them anywhere.

- Actually, I do like prompts because they have made me a better writer.

- Some prompts are outside my writing genre, and no matter how much I try, the words don't flow for example Science Fiction. But that is still not a loss, it helps me better understand the genre I gravitate to.

- Maybe I may not want to write about that particular thing, but usually it is not a problem.

- I don't like the random ones – lists of words – using answers to someone else's questions (that sort of thing.) I don't like the ones that force a genre such as fantasy pictures.

Question 3: What is your favorite type of prompt? Do you have a favorite prompt?

- One where we wrote about our home town.

- Picture prompts are my favorite, I feel that I am not constrained by another's words. My favorite was the "Unholy Cemetery" in Ireland – forgot what it was called. I wrote my favorite story from that prompt.

- Drama! Something exciting that stimulates one's imagination.

- I love picture prompts (photographs or paintings) and lists of words as prompts.

- The short ones.

- Whimsical ideas.

- Pictures.

- I don't have a favorite. It either sparks an idea or it doesn't. Sometimes a picture prompt helps me the most.

- Dark, science fiction/fantasy related.

- I have a board on Pinterest of many different writing prompts, and most of them are dialogue, so I'd say that that's my favorite. I love how just one simple line of dialogue can allow me to come up with an entire story or introduce me to a completely new character. Sometimes, while working on a story, I read a prompt and think, "That's definitely something my protagonist would say," and the prompt works its way into the story in some form.

- Very general. Man, woman, animal, sound, etc.

- Short lists of words to use in a story, and number of words in a story, because it gives me a direction, and it is limiting as well.

- Write a story about a phobia – I chose flatuphobia – the fear of farting in public.

- Short stories, not poems.

- Can't think of a favorite. I like when there are certain words given that you have to include in your story but you still have a lot of license with it.

- Photo that is not genre specific.

Question 4: Have you ever taken a prompt and done something different with it? (example: used it for more than just an exercise) What did you do with it?

- Yes, I entered it in a writing contest and won. (2nd place, but that's still a win, right?)

- My favorite prompt, I wrote a 3000+ word story, I don't think the assignment was to be that long. But the story just flowed.

- No. I am pretty new at this.

- I've entered contests that had prompts, and I've submitted short stories that have come from prompts.

- Not yet.

- No.

- Yes. Wrote a 27,000 short story which is becoming the basis of a novel

- Yes. You know those prompts that say to "write a story based on this image"? Well, I'm currently turning one of those into my first novel. I saw this photo of a girl in an endless green field and it was like her entire life-story played before my eyes in seconds. Now the trick seems to be getting it all from my brain and into my computer!

- Many times. Sent them out to make me some money. LOL

- Wrote a story from the actual prompt as is or used it as the first sentence, paragraph, etc. Also took one work from the prompt and wrote a poem, wrote a story as what happened next from the prompt as the beginning of the story.

- Yes. We had a prompt to write about a situation that turned out completely different than we expected. This lead to an idea for a novel, of which I am 10,000 words into already.

- Yes – worked it into a scene with the characters in my long-term work-in-progress.

Question 5: Do you have any other comments?

- Even though prompts are not my idea, I do find them useful. They get my thoughts flowing and almost always I can come up with something from a prompt. I find that I stick very closely to what the prompt is and do not stray from the actual flow of the prompt. ~ *Esther D.*

- The main thing I have learned from prompt writing is the importance of research. I cannot write about something unless I have reviewed the vocabulary and content that goes with it. Wikipedia is a good source. If I was writing for publication I would have to research the time frame, aspects of people's lives, their cares, clothes, pets, everything. ~ *Louise E.*

- Prompts limit possible story topics from everything. They make writing fiction doable when you just aren't sure what to write about. They are a very useful tool. ~ *Breana E.*

- In general, when you are blocked, a prompt can unlock an idea you didn't know you had. ~ *Vicki G.*

- Prompts are like lingerie for the brain. They stimulate, excite and produce uplifting results. ~ *Christine M.*

CHAPTER SIX

HOW DO WE USE PROMPTS?

There is one basic rule for using prompts: **Use them**. That is the only real rule.

Eco-Friendly

You can recycle a single prompt into an infinite number of works, using a multitude of genres. It can be used for a poem, story, memoir, or anything you feel compelled to write.

The sixth prompt in the anthology section of this book is an example of how one writer, Kerry E.B. Black, used the same prompt and created two very different stories.

Step Out Of Your Comfort Zone

Use prompts to experiment with words in new ways. If you typically write longer fiction use a prompt to trigger ideas for something shorter. Flash fiction (usually under 500 – 700 words) and poetry aren't the only short forms.

Try writing micro stories of 100 or 50 words. Remember that in order for a story to be complete, it must have a beginning, middle, and end. This is also true for the extreme varieties. By practicing the art of minimalism, you can become a stronger writer. Every word must matter. The skill of writing tight enough to fit a tiny word count provides a better polish for your longer pieces.

Similarly, if you tend to write short pieces, try to flesh it out. For example, turn a poem into a short story.

Make It Your Own

Use prompts in any manner you want. You can follow the guidelines or directions provided with the prompt or ignore them. It depends on what you, yourself, want to gain from it. If you are writing to submit for publication or for a contest, by all means, follow the rules.

You can then use the same prompt to write something that you want to write for own satisfaction. In time, you may find a market for the extra piece/s that you develop.

Break ALL the Rules

Don't be afraid to go there. Remember that one rule at the beginning of this chapter. That truly is the only rule that matters.

Break contest rules, like J.J. Hardic did with prompt #12. If there were enough participants who did follow the prompt rule, his story would not have landed in the anthology. However, it provided a good example of how not following guidelines can still lead to publication.

Ignore word count limitations. Linda, a member of one of my writing groups broke the rules for an online prompt and the entire group is glad she did. The prompt was to write a twenty-five word sentence about a picture. Tens of thousands of words later, she's well on her way to completing an intriguing murder mystery set in another time and country. We eagerly look forward to reading each new installment she brings for critique.

Make up words. As writers we have what is known as "literary license" which is the power to create, use, and even abuse words in any way we choose. However, consider your audience. If you are aiming for publication in a refined literary magazine, you may want to confine this sort of creativity to quirky dialogue.

Use verbs as nouns. Feel free to use nouns as verbs. Many nouns are used as verbs and many verbs are used as nouns. This is nothing new. Don't be afraid to use noun and verb words in ways that are not already accepted as common use. Looking at the desk where I am writing I see several examples of words that are nouns used as verbs: paper, pen, phone, and picture are just a few.

Let your dialogue break grammar and spelling rules. Characters need to speak like actual people, not like an exercise from high school English Composition class. As an example, look at the story "Whut Is Dat Shinen Objeck" by Bill McKinley in response to prompt #27. The narrator of the story has a particular way of speaking and the story is written in the form of a letter. Spell check does not like this story at all. It is both challenging and worth the effort to read it to see how a writer can break every spelling rule and still provide an interesting story.

CHAPTER SEVEN

TRIED AND TRUE PROMPTS TO TRY

Over the years I have participated in and led writing groups and classes. Prompts played an important role in each and every one. Here is a sampling of some of the ones which produced excellent results, not only for me but for all of the group members and students involved. Some of these I learned from James Perkins and Andrew Ade in their writing courses. Others I've found or created over the years.

Some are very simple. Others require more effort. Try some, or all, and watch your writing grow.

1 - 10 Words

Write a short story or poem using one word for the first sentence or line, two for the second, three for the third, and so on until you write ten for the tenth sentence or line.

A variation of this prompt is to repeat the process in reverse going from ten words in a sentence or line down to one.

Another variation is to do both of the above for a total of twenty lines, first one word up to ten words per sentence or line, then ten to one in the same story or poem.

50 One-Syllable Words

Write a poem or short story using fifty one-syllable words. It can be done with a topic of your choice. This exercise is more difficult than most people realize. The fifty word limit forces tight writing, and it is hard to use only one-syllable words.

The **extreme** challenge version of the same exercise, do it using each letter of the alphabet as the beginning letter no more than TWO times. 26 letters. 50 words. You can skip a letter or two.

Alphabet Prompt

This is similar to the 1 – 10 prompt. Write a short story or poem beginning each sentence with consecutive letters of the alphabet, beginning with A and ending with Z.

A variation is to write only dialogue with the characters saying one line each with their sentences going from A to Z. Tags may be used at the end of the sentence if needed.

Alternate Endings

Think of a story you like or one you do not. It can be a well known tale or one of your own. Write a different ending. You can change "happily ever after" to "happily never after" or give everyone a brighter future. The possibilities are endless.

Collective Poem

This is best done with a group. Each person writes any two sentences or phrases. All group members provide the others with their lines. Individuals compile the phrases and sentences in any order they choose, then share the results. Use each sentence only once.

Conversation Between Three People:
All Dialogue - No Tags

Without using "s/he said" tags, write a dialogue between three people in a way that your reader will know who is saying what. You can do this by using distinct dialect or accent, by one character addressing the others directly, or in other ways. Be creative. This is an excellent exercise to strengthen your dialogue skills. It is good for playwrights and storytellers alike.

Earliest Memory

What is the earliest event you remember? This does not mean what do you remember because your parents, grandparents, or other adult told you about. Think hard. What is the earliest thing you remember? Describe the memory in detail. Use all of the senses: hearing, sight, smell, taste, touch.

Magazines

There are many magazines written for writers. Explore their pages both online and in print. Most have contests or prompts. One that is frequently used by several writing groups I have belonged to over the years is *Writer's Digest*. They post fresh prompts on their website on a weekly basis. You can write and submit your work, or you may use the prompt however you like. You can find them here:

http://www.writersdigest.com/prompts

Every two months *Writer's Digest* posts a picture or text prompt for a competition. Sometimes they want a short story. Other times they only want a sentence. You may write something to enter or use the prompts in your own way. You can also use past "closed" prompts. You can find them here:

http://www.writersdigest.com/your-story-competition

New Season, New Words

Name
Noun
Verb
Adjective
Adverb

Make up a word for each category. Write a short story or poem using the made up words in each category.

Only Use Your Initials for First Letters

This prompt is very versatile. Using a list of twelve items, write a one word (or more if you choose) for each category using your first initial to start each word. For example, one group I belong to recently used the following list:

Animal
Boy's Name
Color
Drink
Food
Girl's Name
Item in the Bathroom
Movie
Odor/Aroma
Place
Reason to be Late
Something You Wear

Use these words to create a poem or story.

Variations:

In addition to using the words from the list try to use as many words that start with your initial. This can result in a rather humorous piece.

Rather than using only your first initial, use your first initial only for the first item on the list. Then use the last letter of that word to start the next word for the list and so on.

If you are in a group, you can mix things up by passing the papers around with each person adding one word to the list, whether with initials or with last letters as in the exercise above. The story or poem can be written by the first person who had each list or the papers may be shuffled and dealt to allow for surprising results.

Poetry Card Deck

There are many versions of this writing exercise which can be found online. This is similar to one I used in a poetry class.

Using index cards or other similarly sized paper, write one word on each card as directed:

- 8 Crayon Colors (from a box of 64 not the basic 8)
- 8 Pleasant Aromas
- 8 Noxious Smells
- 8 Textures
- 8 Sound Words
- 8 Action Verbs
- 8 Life Forms (such as people or animal words)
- 8 Your Choice

You might want to color code either the paper or the writing instrument you are using to write the words.

The writing exercises:

Shuffle your cards. Deal. Write out the words in the order they appear. Break the lines as you like. They do not need to mean anything.

Rewrite, filling in extra words as desired, keeping the original order. Create a poem that might make sense.

Variations:

- Make a deliberate selection from the words on the cards to create a poem with only those words in a specific order.
- Fill in extra words to create a poem that you can love.
- Use the words to spark a flash fiction, short story, novel.
- Shuffle them, use them one by one, use them all at once or only a select few.
- Use your imagination. It is your only limit.

Scavenger Writing Games

Create a list of items, or find and use a list from the Internet. A simple search will produce many options. Using the lists look for the items and write a poem or short story with the ones you find.

Seasonal Contest

Several writers I know participate in a challenging "24 Hour Short Story" contest. Others use the prompts which are available to non-participants after the contest is over. This contest is held four times a year. You can learn more about it and find a list of previous topics here: http://24hourshortstorycontest.com/ and click on the link to "All Past Topics" at the top of the page.

Three Titles

Write three titles of stories or poems that you will never use. Choose one and use it.

A variation of this is to do this exercise with a partner or group. Each person writes three titles. The other/s write a poem or story. This can be decided by deliberate choose or by writing the titles on paper which is then folded and drawn at random.

Use a Game

Many games have characters. Give the characters back-stories and conflict to create your own stories.

Walk in Nature

Take a walk and explore a park, woods, or farm.
Take pictures.
If there are any wildflowers, gather some.
Press some into a notebook.
Think about the color, shape, etc.
Smell them – describe the fragrance.
Does the aroma evoke a memory? Think about it.
Do the flowers prompt a mood?

More Options to Explore

Pick up some earth.
Be conscious of its weight, texture, and aroma.
Name its color.
Take your time.
Photograph the dirt before/during/after holding it.

When you come back from the walk, write a poem or a page or so about your thoughts.

Be Persistent

Whether you are a new writer or an experienced pro, use prompts to generate ideas. The path to publication can be difficult, but by taking the first steps you can begin the journey. Prod yourself to persist, and you will progress. With progress, you can see your work published.

If you follow the suggestions in this book, you may find yourself:

Prompted to start new writing projects.

Prodded to progress and persist.

Published.

HALL OF FAME

An extra special thank you and congratulations go to a few writers who put forth a tremendous effort.

Here are those who had the most pieces selected from the contest entries, the most creative use of spelling, the youngest, and the only one to have a poem selected.

Top Three Writers

John (J.J.) Hardic	21
Kerry E.B. Black	15
Bill McKinley	11

Honorable Mention

Jenifer McNamara	5
Susanna Fussenegger	4
Louise Eckman	3
Vicki Grey	3
Dana Kerkentzes	2

Most Unique Spelling

Bill Mckinley   "Whut Is That Shinin Objeck" (27)

Youngest

Isabella Sanchez   Age 9

Only Poem

Susanna Fusseneger   "# 19"

PART TWO

THE PROMPTS

In March of 2016 my Tuesday afternoon Write Club helped me come up with the following thirty prompts. The idea was to challenge the members to write a story a day for each day in April.

Due to everyone's overwhelmingly busy schedules, I decided to turn it into a contest.

The list of prompts was given to four local writing groups and made available at a writing conference. It was also shared with a few online writing groups. The included directions were:

Use the following prompts for writing short stories, flash fiction, or poetry. Word limit is under 1,000. (Actually, the shorter your piece is the more likely it is to be chosen. Aim for fewer than 600 words for flash fiction.)

Two or three examples were chosen for inclusion in the anthology part of this book. The purpose of this text is to demonstrate how all levels of writers, from absolute beginner to seasoned professional, can benefit from prompts. Therefore, it was important to have a variety of levels represented.

When I sent the entries out for anonymous judging with some very basic, non-traditional guidelines. They were told to focus on the story as it was told. They had to ignore spelling, grammar and typographical errors and rank them in order of preference for each prompt.

The selected pieces were returned to the writers for revision. The polished results appear in the following chapters after a brief introduction, one prompt at a time.

Prompt # 1

Teenager – Liam
Woman – Martha
Man – Gordon
Setting – Seaside tourist town
Elements to include –ice cream, kites, broken fence, unusual
music, a loud horn

Many prompts offer a set of certain words and key elements which must be included in a story. It is interesting to see how different writers use the same words in different ways. The general theme behind the three stories in this section are similar. The characters and the basic setting are the same in each, but the way the writers handled the requirements varies greatly.

The first is a slice of life with a touch of romance, the second has a touch of science fiction, and the third a bit of fantasy.

As you read, notice the similarities as well as the differences.

Late Blooming
Kerry E.B. Black
(word 957 words)

Martha enjoyed the salt breeze rushing through her hair as she unfurled the kite string. *Who cares if Liam thinks he's too grown for fun at the beach. I'll show him how it's done.* Her son slumped in a disaffected teenage mass on a beach chair, curled around his phone. "Sand will kill it, Mom, just so you know," he had complained.

"Well, I didn't spend two years of savings for you to text your friends. I'd appreciate a little interaction."

"Geeze, why? What do we have in common?"

"What, indeed," she wondered. Since he turned into a teen, the changes in her darling boy astounded her. She had rented kites hoping a little time together along the shore would allow them the opportunity to talk. She shrugged. "Guess this is a parenting fail." Wind whipped away her words as she yelled to him, "We'll go get ice cream in a little bit, okay?" Instead Liam shielded his precious screen and ignored his mother.

A rush of wind sent the kite into a tailspin. It plunged beyond the broken fences into the scrub. Martha jogged along, rolling the kite string as she went. It tangled in the scrub.

A baritone voice startled her. "This must be yours?" He shone like mocha in the sun, shaming treasured images of Hollywood Adonises.

Martha smoothed her knotted hair. "I rented it, actually."

His smile exposed dazzling teeth. "I'm Gordon."

When she took the kite, their fingers brushed. A jolt of electric satisfaction accompanied the impact. "Martha."

His gaze took in her sundress and bare feet, and his eyes shone mysterious as a tide pool in the afternoon. It was not sunburn that colored her cheeks.

"Where are you from?"

"A little town called Russelton in Pennsylvania. You?"

He pointed to his chest. "Local born and bred." His smile broadened. "So, if you're not busy tonight, maybe you'll join me at the street fair? I play with a street band."

Words tumbled from her lips like the haphazard descent of her kite. "I'll have to see. I'm here with somebody, and I don't know what he'll want to do."

"Well, maybe I'll see you later. Enjoy your vacation." When he walked away, she missed his cologne. Spicy like the local cuisine with an underlying cocktail sweetness. She thought, "That probably came out wrong. Might think I'm here with a beau, not a disinterested son." She admired the play of the sun on his muscles before returning to Liam.

Instead of sulking, though, Liam flirted with a bikini-clad girl about his age. She twirled her sun-bright locks and giggled while he flexed his emerging muscles. "Better not intrude," she thought. While she hesitated, he mussed his hair in a self-depreciating movement that reminded Martha of her ex.

He noticed her and waved. She heard him tell the girl, "Be right back," before he ran over the sand to Martha. "Mom, can I have some money?"

"What for?"

"I want to buy Tammy some ice cream."

Instead of protesting her own plans, Martha handed her son some cash. "There's a street fair tonight. Do you want to go?"

His mouth popped open. "Great idea, Mom! I'll ask Tammy." His size thirteen feet kicked up a cloud of grit as he rejoined his date.

Martha bought a new straw hat and sundress from a little shop before returning to their rented bungalow. She found a note from Liam that read, "Meeting Tammy for dinner. Took some cash. Be back late. Don't wait up."

She changed into her new clothes and fixed her hair and makeup. Nothing elaborate. Some mascara and liner to accent her eyes, a tinted gloss on her lips, and a spritz of perfume. "Wonder where the street fair's taking place?" she asked her reflection, regretting her hasty dismissal of Gordon's invitation.

Instead of dining at the pier for seafood, where her lonely state would be evident, she walked the boardwalk and enjoyed fattening, hand-held concessions. Jugglers, fire breathers, and fortune tellers occupied her attention until a cacophony erupted. She peered through a gathered crowd. Gambey dancers hopped, their colorful costumes catching light from the setting sun. Steel drums, a snare, and a fife provided lively, though discordant accompaniment. Martha tapped her foot and clapped when the dancers tipped their elaborate headdresses toward the crowd.

As she turned to head home, a trumpet split through the other street sounds. Martha's heart rate quickened when she recognized the trumpeter. Gordon played a jazzy tune from the age of Bassy. His musical leadership brought harmony to the presentation. The drummers joined in. The fife piped punctuation.

Martha found herself swept up in the dance, swaying like ocean waves and stomping primal percussion. She closed her eyes, threw back her head, and twirled like a gypsy in an old-time movie. The trumpet grew to a nearby crescendo, and she felt an arm about her waist. Gordon whispered into her ringing ears, "I knew you'd come."

"Mom?" Liam's face paled as he approached. His date's lipstick smeared across his lips, giving him the appearance of a clown, yet he crossed his arms in self-righteous indignation. His demeanor broadcasted disapproval, from his squint at her dress to his recoil at her makeup. "What the heck?"

She giggled and shrugged. She thought, "I've done nothing wrong." She snaked an arm about Gordon's waist, mirroring his embrace, and inhaled his spicy scent. "See, son, this is Gordon, and he not only finds me interesting, he even wants to spend time with me."

Gordon pulled her closer to him and winked. Streetlights illuminated mysterious secrets in his eyes, mysteries she intended to explore.

"Liam, be sure to lock the door when you get in. I may be late tonight."

Incident at Cape Carol
J.J. Hardic
(830 words)

When Gordon heard the loud horn at the fire station, he knew that it was too late. He ran outside of his store only to hear the sounds of destruction and carnage. It had finally happened. Nature had struck back at human kind in its most dreadful way, and it took its revenge on the sea side tourist town of Cape Carol.

A woman ran up to Gordon in a panic and grabbed his jacket. "Please, help me!" she pleaded. "It... it came out of the sea."

Gordon heard a roar and crashing. It was a sound he had never heard before, half lion roar, half animal in pain and the town collapsing around him.

"What is your name?" he asked the woman as calmly as he could. He knew she was in shock so he tried to be as patient as he could.

The woman looked around to see if it was safe or maybe if someone else knew her name and would say it for her. "Martha....I think. Yes. My name is Martha."

"OK Martha. Can you tell me what happened? What did you see?"

Terror filled Martha's eyes as she relived the moments. "I picked up my son Liam from soccer practice, we stopped for ice cream, and then it happened. We heard a noise from the pier, then wood breaking, snapping like sticks. Then it stood up and came for us, I ran. Yes. I ran. I told Liam to run.

"Liam. We have to find Liam."

She started to stand, her gate was unsteady; but Gordon eased her back down. "You stay here, I'll find Liam, and you were at the ice cream stand by the pier, right?"

Before leaving Martha, Gordon sent a distress code to his

superiors. They would take control from here. His job was to monitor the marine activity and take water samples. They were already on alert with the past few days' events.

The water temperature had risen ten degrees which was unusual for this time of year. That had brought a migration of whales up to the town and their carcasses where being found on the beach. First one, then more half-eaten blue whales were showing up daily.

For what it was worth, Gordon got a gun from the cabinet and went down Main Street. He turned the corner to see a war zone. The remnants of Cape Carol lay in front of him. Cars were over turned and buildings were in ruin and on fire. Even the fire truck was on its side.

The town's people slowly came out of hiding as Gordon walked through the ruble, they answered the calls for help and uncovered bodies of friends and tourists. Gordon stepped on a mangled metal fence that the thing dragged from the pier. The sign on it read, "No One Permitted Beyond This Point."

Gordon passed what once was the firehouse. Ironically the siren was still going off; but because of the damage to the system, it made an unusual and eerie type of music. It was something you'd hear from a B-horror movie. And that is exactly what this felt like. A young boy stood in the middle of the carnage and destruction eating ice cream.

"Liam?" Gordon asked. "Are you Liam?" The young boy turned and nodded. There wasn't a scratch on him. "Did you see what happened? Did you see where it went?"

Liam pointed to the sky. In the distance a red kite dangled and danced. "Somehow a kite got caught on its horn or something. Just follow the kite."

"Listen. Go to my store, the used book store around the corner. Your Mother is there and she's worried about you. I'll be there shortly."

Gordon started after the thing and turned around. Liam was still standing in the same spot eating the ice cream cone.

Gordon pointed and motioned for him to go. Liam put the rest of the cone in his mouth as he went around the corner.

Gordon followed the dancing kite. It dipped a few times then disappeared out of site. Gordon knew what happened and ran the next block. Cape Carol was perched on a peninsula. The thing had cut across town and went back into the ocean.

For the past year Gordon had monitored the waters and the marine life here. He saw some unusual changes, mutations in some fishes. He knew that the food chain would be affected and it was now a reality. The used book store was a front for his testing lab. He did not want to alarm the people, and there was politics involved.

"Don't scare off the tourists."

It was getting dark and Gordon stared off in the distance of the city lights a few miles across the bay. Would the thing go looking for food? Had it exhausted its food supply at Cape Carol?

Gordon brought up his night binoculars and searched the horizon looking for the kite.

Good Fence
D.R. Sanchez
(970 words)

Martha spent every summer of her life in the same seaside cottage, as had her parents and her grandparents before them. It was good to have something constant in her life, especially now.

The summer after her husband Gordon and teenage son Liam were lost in a tragic accident she went alone to the cottage. It was difficult. She kept imagining that Liam was out in the yard with his father, flying a kite on the beach, eating ice cream, riding his bike. The vision was so vivid that she felt compelled to join them. They vanished as she approached. She blinked hard and slid the back of her hand across her eyes to dry them. She noticed a broken board in the fence where the vision had vanished and squeezed through to the empty lot next door. It had always been empty. Always.

This day it was filled with scores of tiny houses, not like the trend that spawned a television show, more like children's backyard playhouses. They were arranged along carefully designed streets. She noticed shops, a school, and a church, apparently abandoned for decades. Ivy grew over many structures, twining its way up the walls, embracing the chimneys, shuttering the windows. She peered through some windows and noticed that they were all staged with new looking nineteenth century furnishings.

A loud car horn blasted from in front of her house. She remembered the pizza she ordered and hurried back through the fence to pay the deliverer.

After eating, she returned to the yard. The damaged fence board had been replaced. The new piece was held firm. She tried every plank, not one would budge an inch. She propped a ladder against the fence and climbed. There was nothing but an empty lot on the other side. It hadn't been a dream. She was certain. It had taken her twenty minutes to remove the splinter she received when she grabbed the church steeple to steady herself as she turned her ankle in a rut. The wound was hot and angry, in spite of the antibiotic ointment and bandage.

That night her sleep was deep and restless. She awoke several times to find the sheet wrapped tightly around her legs or arms. On one nocturnal jaunt to the bathroom she tripped over the cord of her hair dryer. She knew that it was deep in the back of the drawer, unused for weeks.

When morning arrived, the bruise over her left eye was proof enough that the memory of untying the cord from the towel rack and vanity doorknob had not been a dream. She tried to find a reasonable explanation. It was impossible. Her mind wandered back to when she spent her days with the local kids. She recalled some of the secrets they shared with her.

"Don't you go blabbin' any of this to your folks. We'll have to kill you if you do," Sean O'Brian used to tease.

His sister Brigit wasn't much better, "He's right. It's our duty to guard our old ones. You tell, you pay."

Martha hadn't seen or thought of Sean and Brigit since her tenth birthday. She had a vague memory of news that Brigit had gone to school in the city and never returned and that Sean had gone to war. She stirred herself a fresh cup of coffee and decided to spend the day on the water. She threw a few things into a duffle and pulled on a pair of shorts and a t-shirt over her swimsuit. She didn't care about appearances. She needed to get away for a while, and fast.

By late afternoon, she regretted the hurry. Her makeup had a good SPF level and would have protected her cheeks from the blistering heat. It was a bit cooler in the boat's cabin. She leaned back on the bed and felt herself slip into sleep as the gentle waves kissed the hull.

She dreamed of a perfect life. One spent entirely on her

boat. She was certain she could manage. She knew how to fish and forage, she wouldn't need much. She would never have to go back to the job she despised but kept only because it allowed her to have her summers off. It would take years to build up that much vacation time elsewhere. Strange peaceful music filled her only to be interrupted by a blasting ship's horn. Violent shouting and pounding on the starboard side of her vessel woke her.

On deck, she was shocked to find Sean and Brigit, looking exactly the same as when she had known them as a child.

Sean spoke first, "We know you found our village yesterday. You didn't see us, but everyone saw you, peeping in the windows, stumbling in the streets. We can't let you tell."

"Tell? Who would I tell? Why would I tell?" Martha asked. "Everyone I love is gone. Everyone tells me I'm crazy to not move on." She paused then added, "Maybe I am. I've been seeing things."

"You're no more crazy than I," comforted Brigit.

Martha rubbed her eyes to clear her vision.

"You aren't seeing things, Martha," Brigit continued. "You've grown since we last saw you, but we age more slowly. We've kept an eye on you all these years. We had great fun with little Liam, too."

"The Elders gave us permission to gift you these because you have a special place in our hearts," Sean said as he dumped two burlap sacks on deck.

"What..." Martha started to ask, then gasped as the sacks dissolved and Gordon and Liam stood before her.

Brigit said, "They are yours to keep, but they may never get off the boat. If they do, they will be gone for eternity. Understand?"

Martha nodded, tears flowing freely, cooling the burn.

Prompt # 2

*When I grew up, the worlds of kid
and adult had a very well defined
line separating them. They kept to
themselves, held their secrets, but so
did we. To this day, none of the kids
in our neighborhood ever told
about...*

Childhood is a time of magical secrets, dark mysteries, and adventures that are out of this world. The authors of the trio of short stories for this prompt used memoir style to explore the dark corners that haunt children's imaginations. In each story, the children cover up a dangerous experience.

The first is a peek into the realm of paranormal, complete with the consequences of naively playing with the dark forces behind a Ouija board.

The second imagines the interruption of a typical day of backyard sports. A strange visitation and other inexplicable events are more than the neighborhood kids can handle.

The third story touches on a possible answer to a nationwide criminal mystery.

Children must fiercely protect their secrets. After all, if the adults find out, they would stop the danger...and the fun.

William the Wanderer
Kerry E.B. Black
(920 words)

Kathy hesitated a moment before opening the car door. Her voice sounded tinny and over-bright. "Let's get this over with, shall we?"

Hugh set a hand on her arm. "We should turn around and go home. I told you this is a bad idea."

Kathy shook her head. "No, we have to do this. We abandoned him once. I can't do it again."

"So you believe your stupid dream was prophetic?"

She lowered her eyes and her head drooped. "If you'd have seen him. He looked so lost and vulnerable."

"We never saw him. It's all imagination, y'know."

Kathy glared through tears. "We have to do this."

She unpacked the game, and they entered the house. Drop-cloths covered the furniture, lending the impression ghosts owned the place. Dust collected in corners, and spiders' webs developed complex layers of creation. The floorboards protested their progress, and the stairs groaned at their intrusion.

"Here we are. Looks different, huh? They painted." The third floor room sported no furniture, yet the slanted ceiling and wooden window seat remained distinctive. She sat on the window seat and set the game up beside her. "Well, are you playing?"

"I feel really uncomfortable about this, Kathy. Do you remember how things changed when we'd play? Our parents noticed but never knew why the house got so cold we could see our breath. The lights flickered. Weird noises outside."

"Just stop. Those things were William's way of letting us

know he was here. He needs our help."

"Yeah, but he told us he was a kid. What kid could do all that? Even a ghost kid?"

"He's trapped, Hugh, because he died before he could be baptized."

Hugh rubbed his beard. "Or so he said. I mean, come on, Kathy. This witch board is supposed to be a gateway to the spirit world, but is it really? I mean, someone could have been pushing the planchette. Maybe Timmy Henderson. He was always a jerk and would love thinking he pranked us."

Kathy tapped her polished fingers on the window frame, a clickety click of annoyance. "Timmy Henderson wasn't here every time, now was he? How do you account for that?

"A copy cat? I don't know, Kathy."

"Are you seriously telling me you think all those years were a hoax? I'm telling you they weren't. Now if you'll not help, I'm doing this myself."

"Wait, Kath." Hugh paced, agitation aging his twenty-something face. "Here's the thing. We don't know what we're dealing with. William could be anything. Like on the Internet. You know, a predator poses as a kid to lure a victim?"

"So you think William is a forty year old pedophile getting his jollies through a game board?"

"It's not so far-fetched, is it? I mean, here we are about to summon him again."

Kathy's face set in narrow-eyed dismissal. "As I said, I'm willing to do this alone. You insisted on coming." She sat beside the board. "Besides, I said I have a plan." She reached into a black satchel and removed a Book of Common Prayer.

He shivered. "What's that for?"

Kathy smiled. "A way to help."

"Okay," he said, taking an uncomfortable seat opposite her and placing his fingers beside hers on the planchette. It moved. He whispered, "Tell the truth. Are you moving this thing?"

She pressed her lips into a thin line and scowled at him.

The board spelled out "Hi, Kat. Hi, Hugh. I missed you."

Hugh smothered a cry and shivered.

Kathy said, "We missed you, too. Is this William?"

The planchette squeaked as it spelled out, "Of course. Why were you gone so long?"

Kathy said, "We moved. I am sorry. We're back now, though, to help."

"You promised you would help."

Hugh asked, "How can we help you, William?"

The wooden triangle circled the board as though considering the answer. It spelled out, "Pray with me."

Kathy smiled. "We're going to." She opened her book to 'Rites of Baptism.' "Read with me, Hugh."

The planchette moved on its own. "No."

Hugh froze. His voice trembled. "How'd it do that? Move on its own?"

Wind picked up outside, rattling the glass in its panes. The door slammed shut. Hugh jumped.

Kathy placed her hands on the board and motioned for Hugh to do the same.

"Huh-uh!" He shook his head and crossed his arms. "Damned thing moved on its own."

"Oh, you're ridiculous." The planchette moved beneath her finger tips, spelling, "I know the prayers. Say them aloud." It began to write strange words. Hugh felt dizzy.

Kathy cleared her throat and recited, but not William's words. "Blessed be God, the Father, Son, and Holy Spirit, and blessed by His kingdom, now and forever."

Hugh added his "Amen."

The door flew open and slammed shut again. Hugh shook, but Kathy continued. "There is one Body and One Spirit."

The wind's moans sounded like, "Stop."

"One Lord, One Faith, One Baptism."

A dog howled.

"William, do you desire to be baptized?"

The board fell to the floor, sending the planchette skittering. The wind slammed against the house, puffs leaking through the casement like angry huffs.

A male voice growled, "No."

Kathy made the sign of the cross, closed her book, and gathered her things. She reached for Hugh.

Embarrassed, he noticed his trembling when he took her hand.

Growling menaced from the shadows.

"Time to go." Dark circles dulled her eyes and betrayed their age. "Guess William's what you suspected."

Hugh spat on the ground as they left.

Secret From 1970
J.J. Hardic
(450 words)

When I grew up, the worlds of kids and adults had a very well defined line separating them. The adults kept to themselves, holding their secrets; but so did we. To this day, none of the kids in our neighborhood ever told about what happened to us that day in the summer of 1970.

We were all playing softball, or mush ball as we called it, because the ball was bigger and mushy. You could hit it as hard as you could and it wouldn't hurt if you got beaned by it. We would get up, eat lunch, and play all day, one game after another. They were all pick-up games and we chose players for each game to make it fair.

On July 10, 1970, a strange new kid appeared. He was standing just behind second base. No one saw him; he just appeared there out of thin air.

We yelled at him to get off the field, but he just stood there. And, he wore some strange clothes or uniform. He looked at us and spoke some strange language, we all thought it was Russian or Chinese or something at the time. He had a large forehead, larger than any of us, but we thought he might have had some birth defect. What did we know? We were kids.

Well, one of the bigger kids, Sam, went over and pushed him. We just wanted him off the field. The strange kid didn't say anything; and Sam pushed him again, knocking him to the ground. The strange kid got up and pulled out something from a sleeve or pocket and the next thing we knew they were both gone.

Gone I tell you. Both of them just disappeared.

We all ran home. No one said a word to anyone. Who would believe us?

When Sam didn't come home, we all lied saying he did not play ball with us. His parents called the police and the next few days everyone in town searched for him. The weeks went by and people searched everywhere for him. They went to the abandoned mine close by, the woods, and the creek. He even made the news of a missing person.

The next year at school was tough, sometimes we would all huddle together and talk about it. Where did he go? Would that strange kid come back for us? We were scared for a long time.

Now here it is forty-six years later. The field we played in was bought by some developer who put up apartments and a parking lot.

Yesterday a fourteen year-old boy appeared there, just standing in the middle of the lot. He said his name was Sam.

The Fortuitous Discovery
Bill McKinley
(945 words)

When I grew up, the worlds of kids and adults had a very well defined line separating them. They kept to themselves, held their secrets, but so did we.

To this day, none of the kids in our neighborhood ever told about what we found that summer.

There were four of us that hot day in August 1975: Terry (Neck) Rodgers, Jimmy (Alfie) Lukaszewicz, Ray Hunkele, and me, Mike Uhor. We rode our bicycles almost 13 miles from our homes in Inkster, Michigan via Telegraph Road to Carpenter Lake Nature Preserve in Southfield. We hid our bikes on a deserted path and grabbed our backpacks and canteens that we recently bought at an Army-Navy store. My knapsack was loaded with baloney sandwiches, cup cakes, a Sky Bar, and a bottle of Mission Pop. Although we were all thirteen and would be heading to high school in less than a month, we felt much older and wiser, since this was our third trip on our wheels to the gargantuan park.

We decided to take a different route than our prior treks, when we religiously followed marked trails, climbed manufactured steps and crossed bridges with strangers. As we now deemed ourselves experienced hikers up for excitement, we decided to climb deep into the forest where there wouldn't be any sissies tagging along with parents, uncles, and grandparents.

We had seen the movie *Deliverance* with Burt Reynolds and Jon Voight, so each of us brought along a small pocketknife; we figured we'd be able to "take" any rednecks that might be lurking in the backwoods playing *Dueling Banjos*.

We anxiously departed for the jungle portion of our adventure. Carrying our canteens, we navigated steep hills through numerous trees and thorn bushes, pretending to be Army soldiers in Viet Nam. We pulled resultant burrs from each other's clothes and heads. Those damn things hurt whenever they caught in your hair. Without fail, I had worn my Detroit Tigers baseball cap, but the thorns still managed to catch the back of my head anyway. We spotted shade near a small, gliding creek, not far from a cluster of downed oak trees. We ate a sandwich and drained a large portion of water from our canteens. Several garter snakes slithered by; we threw stones at them. The four of us were "tight" that afternoon. Jimmy eyeballed the relaxing scene. "Man, this is right on! We should do this more often instead of playing baseball every day," he said.

Alfie (we called Jimmy that because he looked like Alfred E. Neuman from Mad Magazine) started to sing *Thank God I'm a Country Boy*, a big hit by John Denver, but Neck said, "I hate that song," and that ended Jimmy's crooning for the day.

We hiked in the thickets and weeds for another hour. It was getting dark, so we decided to head home, because a pesky rain was relentless, and we had exhausted our supplies, save a little water. Our feet hurt, and our clothes were sticking to us like flies on shit. We were drenched from sweat and rain, hungry, thirsty, and laden with long, red scratches on our arms, legs, hands, and faces from the spines of the multitude of rough wild twigs, branches, and copious weeds that we struggled to weave our young bodies past and beneath.

As we walked gingerly down an oily steep slope toward our transportation, the earth under my feet gave way and I fell into an apparent man-made, four or five-foot deep trench that was covered with brush and an abundance of leaves. Ray shone his flashlight into the hole as I struggled to my feet. Maggots were crawling on my hiking boots. "It stinks in here; hurry, get me out," I screamed.

Neck reached down to help me scuttle out of the abyss. Holding my mouth and nose with my left hand, I reached desperately for his. I tripped on something and fell back into the gloomy, slimy pit. The stench made my eyes water. I was ready to vomit. I got up, just as Ray's flashlight started to dim and grow weaker. I looked down to see what I had stumbled on. It was a shoe. Its match was nearby; both had something peeking out.

Ray moved his light to my left and I saw a brown suit, a partially decomposed face with insects, snakes, and maggots slinking out of its eyeless sockets and open mouth with dangling teeth. I grabbed the contents from both shoes, as my buddies helped yank me out of the tomb.

The trio backed away and rubbed their eyes. I pushed the findings into my sack without looking and we backtracked to the cascading small creek we had passed a half-mile back. I stripped down to my underwear and rinsed everything thoroughly.

Back safely in Neck's dad's garage, we dumped my bag. In addition to an ID, each shoe had held two $1000 bills with the picture of Grover Cleveland, the only U.S. President to serve two non-consecutive terms. I had never seen one of those bills before, or since.

Because we were too scared to tell anyone about the body, the four of us made a pact that day to meet every ten years to discuss the incident.

During our fourth meeting last summer, we agreed to meet again this August to deliberate whether it is finally time to tell the authorities about our fortuitous discovery. Without disclosing our mini-inheritance, we could be famous and a movie would possibly be forthcoming.

I have the documentation to prove who is buried on the hillside.

It reads: State of Michigan Drivers License: Issued to James Riddle Hoffa.

Prompt # 3

Wheat was our staple. Everyone grew it in town.
We'd dress it up with things from the garden,
but it was the wheat that held things together.
What I didn't realize was what
the town gave up to keep that wheat coming...

The authors of the following stories followed different paths to the darkness that this prompt suggested. The first has a feel of fantasy blended with a touch of first love and a twinge of something else. The second uses the harsh truths of reality to make a valid argument about the purpose and worth of all aspects of society. The third is a blend of science fiction and dystopian culture disguised with the excitement of coming of age.

All three writers share a common theme. Be careful what you wish for...your wish may come true.

May Day
Kerry E.B. Black
(1296 words)

Winnie braided daisies with her sisters, creating headrails and necklaces for the festival. Springwick, PA celebrated May Day with full old-fashioned flair. Town legends credited the celebration for the success of their wheat crops. Winnie knew nobody believed such things any longer but appreciated the opportunity for a holiday.

Dances, a May Pole, Games of chance, and fortune tellers occupied the day, while bonfires and wilder dancing took place in the evening. Flowers decorated every lamp post. Women wore flowers in their hair. Some donned fairy wings. The men walked about shirtless, even if the weather turned cold. Some placed tribal symbols on their chests with body paints as though revisiting Pictish practices.

Local farmers brought animals for a petting zoo set up in the town center. Winnie loved seeing goats perched atop the gazebo. Her little sisters fed them pellets of pressed food from paper cups while sheep bleated their protests. Twin donkeys pressed their noses to the makeshift fence, conspirators figuring the details of a jail break.

She walked toward a commotion on Main Street. Young men from her school conducted mock battles like medieval knights to decide the King of the Proceedings. She watched with fascination as they struck each other with rattan swords, their only visible armor fencing helmets. The blows left red welts on their bare chests. The crowd cheered when the school football champion, Billy Osborn, received a crown of gilded bay leaves.

The Judge shook Billy's hand. "You get to pick the queen.

Who will it be?"

Billy scanned the crowd. A toothy smile brightening his face when he locked eyes with Winnie.

A sudden heat poured through her, and she dropped her gaze.

Amplified with a microphone, Billy said, "I choose Winnie Culpepper as my queen."

She stiffened, mouth agape. She squeaked, "Me?"

Her sisters joined hands and danced a merry circle around her surprise.

Billy muffled the microphone. "If you'll have me, that is?"

Mrs. Brown, the Mayor, squeezed Winnie's arm. "Oh, what an honor! You know what this means to the town, don't you?" Her grin grew hungry as a feral cats. "Tell him you'll be queen. I'll get you any dress you want."

Winnie licked her lips, suddenly cotton-mouthed. She nodded first to the mayor and then to Billy. "Yes, I'll do it."

The crowd's cheers deafened her, and the Mayor took her to the corner shop for a gown. "Good afternoon, Penelope," she said to the shop girl. "Winnie is to be our queen. Please see to her appointments."

Winnie raised her hands to ward off the attention. "Wait, I don't have much money."

"I told you, my treat. It's the least I can do for the May Queen."

Penelope fussed over styles until they alighted on a princess-cut gown with tiny lily of the valley embroidered along the hem. Winnie's sisters "ooh'ed."

Winnie blushed, pleased with her reflection. "You're sure it's not too close to a wedding dress?"

Penelope bowed, saying, "No, it befits a queen."

"Oh, you look amazing Winnie! We're going to tell Mom and Dad the news."

"Be careful," Winnie said.

Penelope left with Winnie, locking the door behind them. A

welcome committee greeted Winnie as she stepped from the shop. A group of kindergarteners gifted her with armfuls of ribbon-wrapped flowers. The coffee shop presented her favorite drink, double shot mocha latte, in a "fill-forever" cup. "Come back any time today, and we'll refill with anything you like."

Everywhere Winnie went, people smiled and nodded. She beamed responses, waving like a celebrity. "This is so unreal," she whispered to Penelope.

The dress-shop designer smiled. "It's a special day. The King and Queen assure a bountiful harvest. You know." She motioned to the Elite Day Spa. "My friend Dorothy runs this place. She'll want to meet you." Penelope leaned in, bringing with her a puff of sweet perfume. "She always does the Queen's hair and makeup, and she'll be hurt if you don't let her beautify you." She pushed open the ornate door and stepped aside with the grace of a dancer.

Winnie searched the streets, smiling at a waving group of older ladies wearing red hats atop ornate updo's. "I really need to wait for my family. They won't know where to find me if I'm inside."

"Nonsense! I'll keep an eye out for them and let them know where to find you. Don't worry. And here. The chocolate shop sent a box of their amazing strawberries for you. They smell great!"

Dorothy's fingers massaged Winnie's face. The makeup transformed her hum-drum appearance to Hollywood glamour, and her upswept hair dripped with flowers. Dorothy stepped back to admire her work. "I don't think we've ever had a more beautiful queen."

When Winnie stepped to the porch of the shop, a group of townsfolks applauded. Winnie ducked her head as a blush spread across her face. She spotted her mother in the crowd, still and white as an alabaster obelisk. "Momma," she called, waving.

A musky cologne enveloped her, and Billy touched Winnie's hand. The contact felt electric, like static without the pain of a zap. The sun dazzled across his white suit and shining leather shoes. He smiled. "Wow, you look amazing."

Her blush spread under his steady gaze, and her heart skipped, joyful as a dance within her. She whispered, "You look amazing, too."

The crowd chanted, "Kiss her. Kiss her."

Billy licked his lips and looked out of the corner of his eyes. "May I?"

Winnie giggled. "Can't disappoint the crowd, now can we?"

Billy's lips pressed to hers, drowning out the cheers of the town with the pounding of her heart. "What a perfect first kiss," she breathed, tingling.

He wrapped his arm around her, a protective embrace, and rested his forehead to hers. "I've dreamed about you since you first moved here, Winnie. I almost can't believe this is happening."

"Me, either. Do you know what we're expected to do?"

He ran his fingers up her spine, sending thrills of gooseflesh over her body. "This is what we're supposed to do. Personify the Lord and Lady of the harvest."

As the sun set, lanterns brightened the town's center. "Time for the blessing of the fields," announced the Mayor. The gentlemen of town lined the left side of the street while the ladies threw flower petals along the path to the right. Winnie placed her hand in the crook of Billy's arm and strolled to an accompaniment of flutes and drums toward the edge of town and the awaiting fields.

Her mother burst through the line of women, crying, "No, don't do this. Please, Winnie, you're too young."

Three town matrons pulled her back to the sidewalk.

The flowers where her mother knelt, entreating, resembled balled-up writing paper, discarded but missing the waste basket. Winnie's vision blurred, halos encircling the flames. The music grew tinny and distant, as did her mother's cries.

Her words slurred as the cement gave way to soil beneath her feet. "Are we drugged?"

Billy's eyes looked black, all pupil and no iris. "Maybe.

Does it matter?"

"I should go home. My mother needs me."

Billy breathed into her ear, hot and urgent. "I need you." He pressed the length of his body to hers.

She pushed away, surprised by his advance. "Wait, what are you doing?"

"Consummating the field, just like we do every year. Makes the crops grow." Her gown swirled in the starlight, a cloud of innocence, as he scooped her up and carried her to a blanket of flower petals.

"No," Winnie said. Her eyes drooped despite her urgency. "What do you mean, consummating?"

With kisses and passion and prying eyes from the townsfolk glinting in the shadows, Billy demonstrated the meaning.

Wheat Was King
Vicki Grey
(468 words)

The town was small, located near a river, and well-situated for farming. Barges plied the rivers bringing coal to the power plants. Light industry filled the roads with wheat-related products, like feed and flour destined for near and far. Nearly everyone had a job either helping on the farms, transporting the wheat, or manufacturing a wheat-related product so the crime rate was low. Every year people moved in, creating a business district that was easily walked and friendly to customers.

Wheat was king and covered the majority of land north and south of the river. When the wheat was harvested, fields were fertilized to build up the soil for the next planting. This had been done forever. After a while, as the population grew and moved further out from the town limits, complaints began to surface. "Too smelly," they cried. "We can't open our windows when the fields are fertilized." "How are we supposed to have cookouts!"

The farmers tried to explain that it was necessary if they were to continue to rely on wheat and even though their jobs were related to the wheat industry, the people looked down their noses at the farmers. Soon the topic at town council meetings was the inconvenience of living with well-manured fields and tractors or big trucks tying up traffic. Other places didn't have to put up with this nonsense, why should they?

The wheat farmers became tired of being targets for the town folk. They held a meeting among themselves and decided to show the town just how important they were to the economy. They decided to leave the fields fallow.

At first, the townspeople were ecstatic that they were no longer subjected to foul odors from the surrounding fields and no tractors blocked the roads. But without the wheat being planted, quite a few farmhands found themselves out of work and without the wheat harvest, the mills found themselves without a product. Without a product to produce, many factory workers found themselves without a job. Soon the roads cleared of the big trucks that slowed the traffic. With mills shuttered, very few barges were needed to deliver coal to the power plants.

No wheat. No factories. No work. People had to move away to find jobs until nothing much was left of the town.

The next spring, the farmers once again planted wheat. They hired back some farmhands to help out. When the wheat was harvested, a factory started up again and took back some workers. Barges began supplying the power plants. This time though, no one complained about the smell, the truck traffic, or following a tractor down the road. Townspeople now understood that the smell of manure was actually the smell of money and they were fine getting to where they were going a little later.

The Order of Saint Sabatica
J.J. Hardic
(834 words)

Wheat was our staple. Everyone grew it in town. We'd dress it up with things from the garden, but it was the wheat that held things together. What I didn't realize was what the town gave up to keep that wheat coming.

Every seven years the town of Saint Sabatica held a celebration in which a young girl was chosen to join the sisterhood or The Order of Saint Sabatica in honor of the first sister. I was too young at age seven, but at age fourteen I was among the ones to have that Honor.

A three day celebration was held, and we were judged on our health, strength and intelligence. In the end, the sisters chose me. I was taken into the convent, a massive complex of buildings, plazas and fountains. All of the sisters were dressed in black except the High Priestess, who wore red. She oversaw the entire operation of the convent and directed the other sisters in their jobs and chores. Special attention was paid to botany and agriculture. There were several green houses where experiments were carried out to better the wheat. These made the wheat stronger, more durable, because our lives depended on it.

All of the sisters showed the wear of the rugged environment and long hours of work, prayer and meditation. They had to keep the soil rich with minerals and the wheat growing. Their skin was wrinkled with age, some more so than others. I only hoped that I would serve the Order proudly and that someday I would become the High Priestess.

I was escorted into a large stone building that had stood for hundreds of years. It was the final ceremony for induction as a sister.

But I was horrified at what I saw.

There was machinery with knobs and dials and lighted panels. It made a strange humming and beeping sound. In a peculiar way, it was almost musical, but I did not understand anything of what was going on. In the middle of the room was a pool of water with more wires and machines around it. In the pool of lighted water was a woman, old and wrinkled like the rest of them.

The High Priestess came in, explained everything and it terrorized me even more. I tried to escape, but even though the sisters were old and wrinkled, they were strong. They held on to me and one stuck me with a needle. I felt warm and tired, but they held me up. The sisters all circled me, smiling with their crumpled faces. The furrows in them deepened as they smiled at my naked body as they disrobed me.

And so I served the Order and I finally became the High Priestess. That was four cycles ago.

And now you are chosen and I will explain the service your body will provide to the town of Saint Sabitica.

Your body is young, full of nutrients and energy. It is your body's energy that runs this machine called a computer. It is this computer that gives us knowledge in making better, stronger wheat so that we can survive.

It is also this computer that provides the sunlight and keeps this air purified and circulated so that we can breathe.

We are not on the planet Earth. This is something called a space ship. We are traveling through space looking for a new home, a new Earth. We have been traveling hundreds of years and are what is left from something called a nuclear winter.

In this pool are nutrients derived from the wheat. They will sustain you for the next seven years. It is the sisters' responsibility to see that you are nourished and well. These tubes and wires will monitor you and they will take from your body electrical impulses that your mind and spinal column produce.

We found out by accident that occasionally your young

body will climax during certain stages. That is why we have certain spikes in temperatures. You'll be aware of this new sensation, but you'll be in a dream like sleep for the seven years.

The Town has periods of darkness that occur when we undo the wires from the sister now in the pool, and hook them up to you. The computer shuts down for some time, it must reconfigure itself to your body functions and adapt.

The current sister will go to the infirmary for a few months for rehabilitation. She'll get stronger like the rest of us, and then she'll be given a task and responsibility here at the Convent.

Remember this is a great honor for which you have been chosen. It is your body that gives us life, and gives us the chance to find the new Earth.

Four cycles ago I stood in this exact same spot, and now I am High Priestess. I hope sometime during your cycle we find that new home.

Now sleep.

Prompt # 4

I spent way too much time in the library that semester.
With my face stuck in one book or another,
I guess it makes sense that I didn't see her staring at me.
Bill Harris, the librarian, finally asked me about it...

Libraries are an important part of society. They contain and represent the words and ideas that form all of humanity's knowledge. Children who learn to use a library, whether in elementary school, high school, or in their community, have a better chance of being successful in life. There are some who claim that certain libraries are haunted by authors or former patrons. Whether that can be proven or not, it is certain that all sorts of people make use of libraries, including some unusual characters.

The first story in this section takes place in a library. It is short, but there is an intriguing twist.

The second piece is a bit longer and uses the prompt as a point of reference for the events that happen at a nearby bar.

Kindred Spirits
Kerry E.B Black
(368 words)

Daniel considered the painting in its chipped wooden frame. The black and white portrait of the old woman did look different, he supposed.

"What's this got to do with me again?" He asked Bill Harris, the librarian.

"She's Juliette Lowry, founder of this building."

"So you said. What's different, exactly?"

Bill threw up his hands with exasperation. "You are an idiot, aren't you?"

"I certainly hope not. I mean, I've two undergrad degrees and a master's, and I've invested three years of my life working toward my Doctorate degree. I think that proves I'm not an idiot." Daniel tapped his pen against his open notebook. "I'm just not clear on your point."

Bill's words hissed through his teeth like a stage whisper. "She's smiling."

Daniel noticed Juliette Lowry's dimples and bright eyes beneath her Victorian bun and found the effect charming. He shrugged. "So?"

Bill spread open a local newspaper atop Daniel's research. He tapped a photo in the humanities section. "Look at this."

Daniel leaned close. Members of the library board of directors shook hands.

Bill pointed at the portrait hanging on the wall behind them. Juliette Lowry, only more severe in appearance. Firm lines and resolve on an angled face. Different by far than the youthful enthusiasm emulating from the portrait they considered.

"I like the one you've got hanging better."

Bill swung his head ceiling-ward. "That's the thing. It's the same portrait."

Daniel compared the images. "Is not."

"But it is, chum. And I'd like to know why the change."

Daniel shrugged. "How should I know? Anyone checked it for tampering?"

"No tampering, but she's been changing ever since you arrived, spending every day here." He pointed to the table under the portrait.

"That's crazy. Any theories?"

"I was hoping you could tell me what's going on."

Daniel laughed. "How on earth should I know?" His research had consumed his time. Research on the library system. "Wait." However improbable, an answer occurred to him. He set a hand on the table beside his books and winked at Juliette Lowry's gentle approval. "I know." He handed Daniel the hand-written title page of his dissertation. "The importance of the library system to American students, particularly the underprivileged."

Maureen Bizarro
Bill McKinley
(980 words)

I spent way too much time in the library that semester. With my face stuck in one book or another, I guess it makes sense that I didn't see her staring at me. Bill Harris, the librarian finally asked me about it. He described her to me in surprising detail. I admitted I didn't know her.

The next day I was having lunch in a bar and my peripheral vision eyed a pair of shapely legs adorned by a short red dress that plopped down beside me. I didn't look over.

"How are you?" she inquired.

"Are you talking to me?"

"You're the only one within five stools, handsome. Do you think you're DeNiro or something?"

"Wha ... what?"

"Guess you're not a moviegoer. You never saw Taxi Driver with DeNiro?"

"No, I'm not a moviegoer. The last movie I saw was Apollo 13—or was it 14? I didn't enjoy it.

"Look, I know you're the girl who stares at me in the library. Are you trying to pick me up?"

"You're mistaken. I don't go to libraries. I just like to talk to people. I find it interesting. Say, you're not an alcoholic or on drugs are you?"

"Boy, you sure ask a lot of questions, Miss."

"You are! How sad."

"Look, I just came in here for some soup."

"I can drive to you the hospital. I'll do that for you."

"You'll what?"

"My doctor can help you."

"Help with what?"

"Your addiction."

"Addiction? Who said I have a problem?"

"You did."

"No, I didn't"

"That's the hardest part you know?"

"What's the hardest part?"

"Admitting you've got a problem."

"Are you crazy, lady?"

"Me? You're the one with issues. I'm reaching out. I know a psychiatrist who can help you."

"Help me? I don't need help." I looked into her enchanting gray eyes.

"There you go again. Denial."

"Say, I like your perfume."

"Now it sounds like you're trying to pick me up."

"I don't try to pick women up. I was just complimenting you on your fragrance."

"How vain. You don't pick women up, because you think you're so virile they pick you up?"

"Miss, did you skip your morning psychoanalyst visit?"

"So, you like to insult women?"

"No. It just sounds like you have some kind of complex or something."

"Complex? You're the one with problems. It's not noon and you're drinking already."

"There's nothing wrong with a glass of beer with lunch."

"Look, I'm trying to help you and you're being curt with me."

"I wasn't curt. I'm only trying to enjoy my lunch."

"Let's start over. My name is Maureen, and I'm from Ireland. What's yours?"

"I'd rather not say."

"Boy, your problem is a lot worse than I thought."

"What institution did you escape from, Maureen? What's

your last name, Maureen . . . Bizarro?"

"Don't be condescending. I told you my name. What harm would it do?"

"Probably none, but I'm just a private person. I do like your name though. I only knew one girl with that name—when I was a boy."

"Did you get her into the hopper?"

"Into the hopper? What in the hell is a hopper?"

"You know, in the sack—in bed."

"Geez, I was only about nine years old. Do you think I'm a sex pervert, too?"

"I heard you horny Americans shag anything with a skirt."

"I assume by shag you mean you thought I had sex with her. No, I didn't shag her at age nine."

"So you shagged her when you were older?"

"I can't believe we're talking about this irrelevant stuff."

The server interrupts and brings Maureen her soup and tea.

"Where are you from, Mr. No Name?"

"What is this—twenty questions?"

"Twenty? No, I asked a lot less than that. Can't you count? You're so uptight."

"I'm not uptight."

"Well, if you're not tense or neurotic, are you enjoying yourself?"

I put my hands on my chin. "You know, I am enjoying myself. I don't know if I've ever had such an inane but amusing conversation in my life."

"Me too. So, what's your job, No Name?"

"Mums the word."

"I should have known better."

"The Beatles sang that."

"Congratulations to me. Now I know you know something about music. I'm getting warmer."

"I'd prefer to see you when you're hot."

"Aha, here comes the formal pass."

"You sat down—nearly on top of me, as I recollect, Maureen."

"I thought you came in for hot soup, not a hot woman."

"I'd much prefer the latter."

"Don't even think about it," she said. Then, gazing into my eyes with a sexy smile, Maureen leaned in closer and whispered, "How was the soup? Was it as good for you as it was for me?"

"G ... great. You have good taste."

"Except in strange men."

"We all have our cross to bear."

"Does that mean you're religious?"

"No, I'm not."

"Oh, my God. I actually found something else out about you. Was that a slip up?"

"No, you're wearing me down."

"Progress is good. Wow! We've been talking for over two hours. I must leave."

"Do you have an appointment?"

"Yes."

"I thoroughly enjoyed the healthy conversation, Miss Bizarro."

"Ditto, Mr. No Name. I think you're a riot."

"Here's a stupid question for you, Maureen. Will I see you again?"

"Maybe I'll see you here tomorrow—no promises." The tall, shapely, and alluring woman strolls out. As she opens the door, she turns, waves, and blows me a sensuous kiss.

******

I went to the library and restaurant every day for the next three years. I never saw her again. I'll never know if she was the woman that Bill Harris said stared at me—not that it matters.

I just can't get her out of my mind. Perhaps she was right. Maybe I do need a psychiatrist.

Prompt # 5

Mom handed me the last box from Gran's attic.
"Done," she announced, with some triumph.
"Ice cream?" I reminded her of her earlier promise.
"Sure – grab me the broom when you come back up here."
I nodded and began my trek down four levels of stairs
when Mom's gasp brought me running back up the steps.
"Andrew," her face was grey. "Come look at what I've found..."

While photographs were not a part of this prompt, each of the authors in this section included them in their stories. Some people say that a picture is worth a thousand words. Others say it paints a thousand words. In reality, a picture can prompt thousands of stories.

A photo captures a split second of time. What happened before? What happened after? The memory of the event frozen by the camera is shared by those who experienced it, yet it is different for each of the participants. The reality is that there is no reality, or rather that there is no singular reality.

Open a box of memories. Read the stories as told by the contents. Create your own versions.

Proud Discovery
Kerry E.B. Black
(325 words)

Andrew Proud hauled the box labeled "Photos" down the ladder, adding it to the wall of boxes he'd stacked. Mom's tidy script told the contents. Christmas decoration. War memorabilia from when Great grandpop fought with the Union during the Civil War. Andrew grabbed the broom as his mom had instructed and ascended the rungs with the grace of a monkey.

From the attic came a gasp, then a trembling call, "Andrew?"

He paused, heart sinking, and nearly missed a rung in his haste. "Mom, are you okay?"

Tears left tracks in the dust speckling her cheeks. "You're not going to believe what I've found."

He thrust aside the broom and rushed to where she knelt beneath a window. She asked, "Do you remember the stories Gran used to tell, about ghosts scuffling in the attic?"

Andrew trembled. "Yeah. Used to creep me out. People singing to the stars and scraping about over her head."

Mom shook her head. "Her room was just below where we're standing, so it makes sense."

"What does? What are you talking about?"

She pointed to a spot where she'd removed a floorboard.

He earned a splinter as he wrapped his fingers around and removed another. He squinted into the gloom. "There's something here," he said.

"I think so, too."

They worked together until they found steps. A secret

room. Artifacts from the 1800's. A basin and linen. Tin cups. A pitcher and platters.

"What do you think it means?" Andrew asked, running a finger along a broken leather and iron tether.

A puff of dust rose as she sat on the edge of an ancient cot. "I think it means we should be proud of your great grandparents, Andrew." She blew dust from the top of a sheet of parchment and smiled. Signatures and X's beside antebellum dates. She held out the page to her son. "I think it means our family home was a stop on the Underground Railroad."

A Picture of Life
Louise Eckman
(329 words)

Mom handed me the last box from Gran's attic.

"Done," she announced with some triumph.

"Ice cream?" I reminded her of here earlier promise.

"Sure — grab me the broom when you come back up here."

I nodded and began my trek down four levels of stairs when Mom's gasp brought me to a halt.

"Andrew," her face was grey. "Come look at what I've found...."

Without grabbing the broom, I hustled back up the stairs.

"Andrew," she said in a measured tone, "this is my father...and your grandfather."

Surprised, and a bit scared, I looked at the large photo she showed me. A man's name was written at the bottom of the page – it said Jake.

My mom had told me a few times that she never knew her father. He disappeared during the Vietnam war – he went missing in action. She was a baby when it happened.

Mom started to breathe faster, and then tears began running down her cheeks. She let the photo slide to the floor and held her head in her hands.

I didn't know what to do, but I knew I shouldn't mention the ice cream.

"Let's take the photo downstairs, Mom," I said.

She picked up the photo and we walked down the narrow, dusty stairs to the first floor. Gran's house had been empty for a long time.

She carefully placed the photo on the kitchen table, and we

sat down in the old, wooden chairs. The man in the photo looked friendly and smart. A bit of pride swept through me; it was the first time I ever thought of him as a person.

"Oh, Andrew," she said with emotion, "this is the first photo I have ever seen of my dad!"

"Good, Mom," I said, and I leaned over to the cooler to check on the ice cream. There it was – perched on a bag of ice along with some bottled water.

"Let's celebrate with the ice cream," Mom said.

Medals
J.J. Hardic
(679 words)

Mom handed me the last box from Gram's attic. "Done," she announced with some triumph.

"Ice cream?" I reminded her of an earlier promise.

"Sure. Grab me the broom when you come back up here."

I nodded and began my trek down four levels of stairs when Mom's gasp brought me running back up the steps.

"Andrew." Her face was grey. "Come look at what I found."

She turned and showed me an open box full of army medals. I immediately recognized one as the Purple Heart given for bravery and being wounded in combat. There were pictures of Grandpap in uniform.

"Somehow he survived World War II," Mom sighed. "He never did talk about it much, not here anyhow. He'd go to the Club with all his war buddies. That's how they dealt with things in those days. Now everyone sees a therapist."

"I'd like to look at these pictures Mom. Maybe I can scan them into the computer and make an album for the family."

"That would be nice."

I forgot about the ice cream and spent the next two hours sifting through the photos of the war and the exploits of my Grandfather. Infantry man, Michael Hunter. Enlisted at age nineteen to fight for America. Saw Europe mostly by foot.

Incredible.

I was able to put together a slide show with letters he had written along with the photos. And then one night while watching it, something very strange happened. I must have fallen asleep at the computer while the slide show was going, but it seemed so real.

I closed my eyes for a few minutes, and I heard thunder and rain outside. I could feel the cold wetness of the rain being blown in and then a loud crack of thunder. When I woke, I was in my house; but there was a hole in the roof and the rain was coming down on me.

I heard the pops of guns and large vehicles. I went down the creaky steps to find a barrage of activity. Military men were evacuating the place, carrying maps and boxes of letters. Someone kept yelling to get out, the Germans were coming. They were a few kilometers away. Then an explosion hit and people went flying everywhere.

Yells for medics went out. There were casualties in the head quarters. An older man took charge and ordered the men to defend the bridge leading into town. We needed time to triage the wounded and get them out.

He came over to me and grabbed my dog tags and looked at me straight in the eyes.

"Son," he said. "We may need your blood, you're the universal donor."

He pointed to a cot. "I'm not going to order you, but you can save someone's life if need be."

I went to a table and lay down. One of medics put a band around it and stuck me with a needle. I watched my blood fill up a bottle and then I fell back to sleep.

I felt myself falling and woke back up in my house, sitting in my chair. The slideshow had come to an end. I went down stairs and found my mother reading a letter.

"You may find this interesting," she said. "Your Grandpa was in some fight in a town in France. A bomb hit the town and he, along with some guys, was hurt. One young man was badly injured and told the medics to take all of his blood and to give it to the others. He knew he was going to die and he wanted to save as many of the other solders as possible." My Mother looked up at me. "You know, if it weren't for that brave young man, your Grandpa would not have made it home; and you and I would not be here."

I know it's not possible for me to have been there. But how did I know that story? It wasn't on the computer slide show, and that was the first time I had seen the letter.

Prompt # 6

She saw it out of the corner of her eye.
A shadow outlined by porch light.
She knew there would be a perfectly
good explanation for it and yet...
a chill ran through her body.

This prompt led the authors into the darkness of myth and the supernatural.

It is also proof that not only do different people see and use the same prompt in very different ways, but also that one person can use one prompt to produce numerous stories.

One person wrote the first two stories in this section. In the first, myths of shape shifting and evil lurk in unexpected places. In the second, a woman confronts the wrath of a fairy after a lifelong pursuit.

The third story deals with death, memories, and a stubborn car.

Humans have long lived in terror of the unknown that hides in darkness. It was important to be afraid of predators and enemies. Without this trepidation, no species can survive. Feeling fright is not the sign of a coward. It is a sign of intelligence. History and legends are full of those consumed with fear. When they dare to face the horrors they dread, we call them heroes and villains. Yes, villains are also subject to fear.

Colleen's Visitor
Kerry E.B. Black
(321 words)

From her clients' erratic behavior at the assisted living home today, Colleen decided tonight must host a full moon. She pulled her scrub shirt over her head and tossed it in the laundry basket before pouring a glass of red wine.

The day presented a number of challenges, but the worst involved little Jimmie Fetterman. He had complained of invisible itches and, when she attended another boy, he scratched deep, bloody gouges on his arms, neck, and shoulders. By the time she retrieved the health kit to tend the wounds, Alroy Lobo was licking Jimmie's arms. When pushed away, Alroy had growled like a demon, "Bitch!"

Colleen closed her eyes, begging the warmth of wine to deaden her recollections and caress her throat. Before being restrained, Alroy had grabbed for Colleen. His fingernails left tracks on her neck. He had licked her blood from his hands, threw back his head, and howled.

She swallowed another sip from her goblet, draining it.

As the sedative took effect, Alroy had stared at Colleen through the tangles of his dark hair. "I'll see you tonight." He licked reddened lips.

Banging outside drew her attention. The garbage bins clattered down the driveway. "Darn it!" She yelled, flicking on the porch light. A movement and a shadowy dash drew her gaze. A huge dog panted at the end of the walk, its eyes reflecting the porch light.

She tapped her wine goblet, grateful for the barrier of the screen door. "So you're the one who keeps knocking over my trash bins."

The dog licked its lips.

She shivered despite the warmth of the night. She did not recognize the long-legged canine. It bore the appearance of desperation and neglect. Without knowing why she said it, Colleen's voice trembled, "Alroy? Is that you?"

The beast threw back its head and howled. It wore no collar or tags, just dark, tangled fur the same color as Alroy's hair.

Facing the Beast
Kerry E.B. Black
(499 words)

Belinda recognized it, skulking in the peripherals. Rationality told her it was nothing, a trick of the porch light and fog, yet a chill ran through her. It had tracked her, as her mother warned it would. The thing hoped to complete its task. Its kind disliked being thwarted, after all, and immortality conveyed a strange patience.

An owl's hoot echoed, and with a hushed rustle of wings, it scooped up a screaming rabbit in its talons. The prey's shrieks fell silent as the own disappeared from view.

Belinda shuddered, sure of the truth. It had found her, after all these years, tracked her from one coast to the other. She tipped back her head, allowing silvered hair to spill between her shoulder blades. With studied nonchalance, she returned to her mobile home and latched the door. Its steel reinforcement could do little to prevent the thing's entry. She pressed her silver locket to her lips and breathed a prayer as she gathered the items her mother had assembled, items she hoped Belinda would never need to use, since they were of uncertain helpfulness.

The thing outside howled, mournful, alerting its mistress of its trapped quarry. Belinda. Daughter of Thomas, who fell under the spell of a fairy maiden. Despite being pregnant with Belinda, her mother Maeve followed Thomas into the enchanted land and demanded his release. The fairy king admired Maeve's courage and took uncharacteristic pity. He allowed the couple to go free. The fairy maiden continued to desire Thomas, though, and began a hunt.

Belinda knew the story. Her mother repeated it every night, explaining why their family lived like gypsies, why Belinda attended no schools or maintained friendships. When the night wind brought sounds of primeval growls, they moved. Shifts in grasses betrayed scouts. Elfshot rained around them, and danger came with eddied breezes.

Belinda wore her clothing backwards and inside-out. She tucked lucky clovers in pouches, wore a silver locket, and carried an iron dagger pressed against her calf. Prayers and holy water became mantras and salvation. She grew old, though, and her parents died.

Belinda knew nothing but flight, nothing but a primitive desire to escape. She'd heard of stable lives where fear didn't flavor every meal and haunt dreams. Tonight, she would embrace her fate and hope she could spend the rest of her life sitting still. She removed the locket and placed it with her mother's other protections. She slid the knife beneath the satchel and opened the door.

"Sorry." Belinda addressed the glowing gold eyes of the beast. "I'll not run any longer. I'm too old." She sat in the doorway, hugging her knees to her chest. "Get on with the killing if you must."

The beast bared knife-sharp fangs. Its fierce mistress stepped from the shadows and rested an alabaster hand upon its head. "Ach, without chase, there is na hunt. If ye don't run, we canna chase." She narrowed feline eyes in an angry glare. "Fine. Be off wit ya, then."

Ginger's Gift
J.J. Hardic
(701 words)

She saw it out of the corner of her eye. A shadow outlined by the porch light. She knew there would be a perfectly good explanation for it and yet .... A chill ran through her body.

How did it get here?

She was home all day and did not hear it. No one knocked on the door and said that they brought it back, for whatever reason. But, there it was, Dad's 1971 Black Corvette.

Ginger took a deep breath.

"There has got to a logical explanation for this. I just can't think of one right now," she told herself. Ginger went back inside the house and looked at the clock. The dealership was closed now. "Maybe they decided they didn't want it after all. It still needed a lot of work to be done. I'll call them in the morning."

Ginger thought about the Corvette. When Mom died, Dad all but went to pieces. He became depressed and spent most of his days drinking beer and staring at the television. It got so bad that he stopped paying the bills. That's when Ginger moved back home and took over the household.

Her father always liked cars and did a lot of work on them himself. He always said the dealerships over charged. So, he did his own oil changes, brake changes and generally fixed whatever ailment the car had. He did the same with Ginger's car too.

One day, while Ginger took him for a routine doctor's appointment, he spied the car sitting in front of a junk yard. Tires flat, windows yellow and stained, taillights gone, but Dad fell in love with it. After the doctor's appointment, they stopped; and, before Ginger knew, a tow truck was hooking it up and it was in the driveway.

Working on the car filled a void in his life. He always had a plan, a next step and he searched the junk yards and Internet for parts. Some days he would spend hours working on something. On other days, a retired friend would come by and he'd show his friend what he had done. They would talk about everything, but mainly what Dad was going to do next on the car.

Fixing up that old beat up car gave him purpose again.

All that changed when he had a heart attack in the garage. Ginger went out around nine o'clock to check on him, but he had been dead for a few hours. He lay on the cement with a screwdriver in his hand. Now he was with his wife.

* * *

The next morning Ginger took a break at work and phoned the dealership.

"I thought you changed your mind and took the car back," the salesman said.

"No. I thought you didn't want it and brought it back."

There was an awkward silence on the phone. Ginger did not want to get into an argument with the guy over who brought it back and for what reason. It was Dad's car and Dad was not here to work on it. She just wanted it gone.

"O.K. Look, I don't know how it got back to the house, but please come get it. I have no use for it, and I certainly don't have the time or knowledge to finish it."

When Ginger got home, the car was gone. She ate some dinner and cleaned up; then watched a little television. She checked her e-mail and took out the trash. It was garbage day.

She saw it out of the corner of her eye. A shadow outlined by the porch light and a chill ran through her body again. There it was again. The black 1971 Corvette her Dad was working on.

Ginger dropped the trash bag and held her breath. She slowly walked over to the car, touched the fiberglass frame, and nodded.

"It's okay Dad. I get it. You want me to have the car. You

were working on it for me. I'll call the dealer and leave a message telling him I changed my mind...again. I'll finish it."

A tear rolled out of Ginger's eye and dropped on the car.

"Or we'll finish it together."

Prompt # 7

Fat, brown, wiggly it had shown
up at the house early that morning.
"Can I keep it, Mom?"
"Get away from it! Now!"

Children are either fascinated by or terrified of creepy crawly creatures. Frequently they are both. Under normal conditions, getting the chance to observe the multitude of the smallest of animals is a rewarding educational experience.

However, in the stories that follow, the lessons learned may not be beneficial to the living. The first story delves sweetly into the realm of horror. The second is a glance into a possible future world.

The lesson is the same in both stories. Beware of the things that follow you home.

Casimir
Kerry E.B. Black
(434 words)

Adelle backed away until the kitchen counter arrested her retreat. She gripped its wood, grateful for its solid reality. Her voice quaked. "Jeremy, where'd you get that?"

Her son stroked it along its spiny back. It arched up to his touch and sort of purred. It revealed startlingly sharp teeth in a twisted smile, its tiny eyes glinting with inhuman knowledge.

Jeremy's grin revealed missing front teeth. "Isn't he cool? His name is Casimir."

Adelle's knees gave way, and she slid to the floor.

Jeremy's brow crinkled with concern. "Mom, are you okay?"

The thing squirmed in Jeremy's grip, stretching its claws toward Adelle.

She screamed, "Get that thing out of here right now!" She did not mean to yell, but terror gave her voice irrationality.

Jeremy cocked his head to better view the wiggling grave-brown mass. Jeremy's thin arms could not contain it, and sharp-ended limbs dangled. With each exhale, its ribs protruded.

Using the rational voice he reserved for his kid brother, Jeremy said, "It's hungry, Mom. I think it needs us."

The thing winked.

Adelle squeezed her eyes to shut out the sight of her six-year-old holding a nightmare from her childhood. She remembered the one she rescued. It had needed her, too. The same stench of decay enveloped its skin, and it told her its name. How else would grade schooler come up with Casimir? Mom and dad allowed her to keep it in the shed where they stored the lawn mower and weed whacker. It had snorted at oats and fruit, but it devoured meat. Although it never fleshed out, it grew. Its legs lengthened, and its snout elongated until it no longer fit in the shed. With tearful eyes, six-year-old Adelle had set it free.

It had tossed its head, sending a strangle of mane to waft from its neck, and screeched. With the speed and grace of a spider, it scaled the side of the house to her parents' third floor room. Their screams haunted her still.

She shivered, opened her eyes, and saw love radiating from her son. She whispered, "Guess it's the time of atonement."

"Mom?" Jeremy stepped forward, concern distorting his face. "Please, can I keep Casimir? Please?"

She stretched out a hand toward the beast but recoiled, unwilling to touch it. "Are you my Casimir's offspring?"

It nestled its face into Jeremy's neck like a bashful infant.

Jeremy blinked sincerity. "I really think it needs me, Mom."

Adelle pulled a steak from the refrigerator and chopped it into uneven chunks. "You can keep it outside in the shed where I store the lawnmower."

Not Wanted
J.J. Hardic
(1000 words)

Fat, brown, wiggly. It had shown up at the house early that morning.

"Can I keep it, Mom?"

"Get away from it! Now! Get in the house and radio for Tom. Do it quickly!" Kayla yelled. It was more out of fear and anxiety rather than for something her son had done wrong.

This was the second one that showed up in the small colony. The first one got onto a chicken. It left only macerated bones and feathers before the family killed it. It sent alarms through the colony as yet another unknown the hostile planet threw at them.

A jeep pulled up in minutes and a team in biohazard type suits pulled up. The Team circled it with a cage and nudged the slow moving, two-foot long, caterpillar like creature in. Tom took off his helmet and approached Kayla.

"Are you and Ivan alright?" he said out of concern.

"I'm just shaken up a bit. Since Ray's death I have been on edge with everything on this planet. I know we've been through this before, but I think we need to consider moving on. We're not wanted here Tom."

"I know that Shane will find this interesting and he'll want to study it, but I'll call a town meeting and we can voice our concerns and maybe vote on something."

"If this is anything like our caterpillars back on earth, I don't think I want to be around when it becomes the other thing." Kayla and Tom stared at the two-foot long furry thing wiggling around in the cage.

"I'll call the meeting for tonight," Tom reiterated.

The colony started off with two hundred and thirty five and they were down to one hundred and sixty. A few deaths happened over the years of travel which was bound to happen, but this hostile world was claiming bodies more and more.

First it was the weather, the harsh climate; then it was nutrition and food. But now the planet was striking back. The plants were inedible, the water, when they could find any, was loaded with minerals and sulfur. It always had that rotten egg smell.

But the Pilgrims endured to this point at least.

Doctor Shane McNepson stood and spoke. He addressed the crowd in the cargo bay of the main ship they came in.

"We all share your concerns Kayla, but look how long it took to find this world. And yes, there are hardships and unforeseen things happening here, like your husband; but we can adapt. We can make this work for us.

"Tell me, how many of you are willing to give up on everything we have done here? We have built homes and started a new life."

A handful of people raised their hands. Shane extended his arms to say he had won the argument. No one was giving up or leaving.

"Yes, my husband, as well as countless others, died here. How many lives will it take for everyone to understand that we are not wanted here? This planet does not want us. It's fighting back. My husband was walking along a rock formation when a geyser exploded from underneath him.

"Now we have these two foot long caterpillar things. Who knows what monstrosity it will turn into it?"

Tom stood up next to Kayla.

"Would the colony be willing to give up a small ship to Kayla and the others who want to leave?"

This question brought up a heated debate over the colonists being unified and what was best for the colony. Others joined Kayla and Tom in wanting to leave. Thirty people decided they did not want to stay.

A vote was taken and it was decided that the protestors could leave in search of another planet suitable to their liking. The remaining stronger colonists would conquer this world. They could take the provisions they had already saved and whatever anyone wanted to donate to their failed mission.

The next week more of the caterpillars showed up. They attached themselves to trees, the houses and spun cocoons around themselves. The one previously captured had made its own cocoon in the cage and lay dormant.

Hours before takeoff, Kayla and Tom looked at the new cocoon on her house. She was very uneasy about this and took her son to the ship. Others were already on board and loading supplies. They stopped by Shane's to pick up a few more fruit bearing plants that would help with the air and food.

Shane was not at his desk so they went in the back where his plants and other supplies were kept.

They heard a crashing sound and a rhythmic pumping sound. They carefully made their way to the back, calling his name.

Kayla screamed but Tom covered her mouth and held her tightly. There, leaning up against the shelves, was Shane. He had knocked over plants and supplies.

On his back was a three-foot long insect like creature with a long wingspan. Its abdomen had some type of stinger in it. The stinger appeared to be pumping some type of venom into Shane's body. Two large mandibles held his neck intact.

Shane stared at them. He wore a hopeless expression on his face. He seemed to be asking for help. Tom slowly backed away and out of the storefront.

"Run to the ship. Prepare to blast off. I'm going to sound the alarm and I'm right behind you."

As Kayla ran, she heard the sound of the alarm. Seconds later Tom was in sight and once aboard she closed the hatch door.

She saw a crowd run toward her. The flying monsters had burst through their cocoons and were attacking the rest of the colony.

"Emergency takeoff!" she yelled through the loud speaker. "Thirty seconds!" She strapped herself and her son into the seats. Tom was beside her.

The engines roared and the ship lifted off the ground incinerating the colonists banging on the hull with monstrous insects attached to them.

Prompt # 8

He drove, looking neither left nor right.
His hand held the wheel in a death grip.
Faster, then faster still...

The urgency promoted in this prompt led to a common theme in the stories selected. Each is a matter of life and death. Beginnings and endings. Possibilities and finalities.

Focusing on a prompt is like focusing on any aspect of life. It is important to pay attention to the details and consider all possible outcomes, even if a life isn't at risk.

Escape
J.J. Hardic
(691 words)

He drove, looking neither left nor right. His right hand held the wheel in a death grip. Faster, then faster still, until the pain in his left arm began to throb.

"Aahhh!"

He slowed down and took a few deep breaths; then glanced at the bloody shirt he wrapped around his left arm. Waves of smoke passed before him and sifted in the vents. He coughed several times and sped up again.

"I can make it. I can make it," he coughed.

As the car wound its way around the curve, a burning tumbleweed hit his door sending sparks and embers everywhere.

"I have to make it. I have to make it."

Carlos thought of his wife and daughter and hit the gas pedal. Getting to the bridge was his only hope of survival. The river was a natural barrier and the firemen were working that side.

Carlos had sent his family on ahead only hours earlier. He had stayed behind like some others to try and save their house. They made so many memories in that house. He had hosed down what he could, loaded up what he could, cameras, photos, albums, work things, clothing...... his daughter's favorite doll.

No. He didn't have time to get Renalda's doll. She would burn with everything else. He waited as long as he could, maybe too long, that's when the burning tree fell and the hit his arm. The impact of the tree and the fire seared his skin; but it also cauterized the wound. It hurt like hell, but he had to keep driving. He had to keep pushing before the fire or smoke engulfed him.

Carlos saw a sign for the bridge one mile ahead. It would be a race between him and the inferno. Carlos glanced out the window and saw the blaze along the side of the road. It was also on the hillside to his right. The smoke got thicker and another burning tumbleweed hit the windshield, bursting like an explosion.

Carlos slowed the car as the road got harder to see, and then it disappeared.

He did not know where he was and the smoke was filling up the car. He covered his mouth and coughed again.

It could not end like this. So close to safety and so very far away.

There were two things he could do. Gun it and hope for the best; or go slow and hope that he did not die from smoke inhalation.

Carlos went ahead, slow at first waiting for any sign that the car was off the road, but that never happened. Carlos heard a thud and the car came to a complete stop. He hit something. It was either the side of the hill, a rock or another car.

Carlos coughed again and laid on the horn. Hopefully someone would hear it.

Carlos had no concept of time but he coughed again. His eyes were watering from the smoke. There was a tapping on the window and a fireman was standing there.

"You alright buddy?" the fireman shouted.

Carlos opened the door. He was in the middle of the bridge; his car had hit the cement barrier separating the sidewalk and road.

The fireman put an oxygen mask on his face.

"You got lucky pal. We heard the car horn beeping and then the winds shifted." Carlos started to say something but coughed again. "Take it easy. We got a stretcher coming for you. Let's get you in the ambulance and take care of that arm. Then we can get your car off the bridge and see about calling someone for you."

As Carlos lay on the stretcher he felt the wind and watched as it moved the smoke away from the bridge. The thick cloud hung above what was left of the smoldering forest. The landscape was scarred with burned trees and black ashes.

Such beauty, yet such devastation.

Carlos closed his eyes and took a few more deep breaths. He clasped the fireman's hand in heartfelt handshake. He had won. He had escaped the fire and the smoke. He would soon see his wife and daughter.

Some Things Just Can't Wait
Virginia McBurney
(346 Words)

He drove, looking neither left nor right. His hand held the wheel in a death grip, faster, then faster still until he finally saw the hospital, slowed down, and drove toward the emergency room entrance with his horn blazing LOUD and LONG. The nurse came running out to the car, looked into the open window asking, "What's wrong?"

The man answered, "My wife is having a baby!"

The nurse opened the back door, checked the mother stretched out on the seat, and saw that she was crowning

"I'll be right back," she said as she ran into the E.R. office to get her small delivery packet, including delivery instruments. Back out in about thirty seconds, she opened the packet, then told the mother, "Push."

Slowly the baby's head, then the rest of her body emerged. The nurse held the baby by her ankles upside down, and took a small cloth from the packet to wipe the mucous out of baby's mouth. The nurse gently rubbed the baby's back up and down to get her breathing, and soon crying. The Nurse laid baby on mother's abdomen, and then got the two clamps and scissors from her packet. She put one clamp on the umbilical cord next to baby's abdomen, left a small space, put the second clamp on the cord, and cut the cord between the clamps.

The anxious father was watching all of this quietly. The nurse asked him, "Please hold this clamp near the end of the cord, and don't let it open, or your wife will bleed. I'll take the baby into the hospital and call for help for your wife."

As the nurse entered the ER door, the night nurse supervisor had just arrived to see what was happening. She took the baby, while the nurse called for help, which arrived quickly to wheel the mother into the hospital where the Doctor could then deliver the placenta.

Soon the father was able to see his baby in the nursery, and his wife resting in her room. All was well.

The Final Game
Bill McKinley
(618 words)

He drove, looking neither left nor right. His hand held the wheel in a death grip. Faster, then faster still, Myles Grundler drove until he reached the park down the block from her house.

He trudged down the street, the leather knapsack, a gift from Barb, weighing down his arthritic left shoulder.

Only an hour earlier, he rudely waved the server away and downed his third cup of black coffee without raising his glassy eyes from the telltale newsprint. His psyche told him this day was imminent, but his unpersuasive heart told him otherwise. "Seventeen years, seventeen years," the 57-year old, self-made billionaire had mumbled inaudibly, as nearby patrons gawked.

"Back up on the curb, Buddy, until I tell you to step off," the self-important cop shouted from the other side of the street. Unfazed by the ill-natured order, the silver-haired, bewildered man did as commanded. Waiting for the lengthy light, his life flashed before him in a fleeting minute: *an only child; captain of the high school and college football, basketball, and baseball teams; star pro quarterback; founder of several successful multi-million dollar companies; married the girl of his dreams at age forty; and, former councilman and mayor.*

Feeling light-headed, he entered the park and found temporary refuge on a worn, paint-chipped bench near the slides and waterfall. As he watched gleeful children run by numerous times with inattentive abandon, Myles' lingering conviction that his lone failure in life was directly related to kids—his inability to produce one—tugged at the former superstar's manliness, and his head started spinning, akin to the small silver ball circling a roulette wheel. Unlike the steel sphere, however, this man knew not only the destination of his instant spiraling journey; he had pre-planned exactly how it would end. There would be no winners at the culmination of this game, because house rules applied today, and the ex-jock wrote them mentally well in advance.

The arguing, pleading, and talking stages had concluded fruitlessly. The classes, workshops, church group discussions, and analyst visitations were monumental disappointments, too. Now, there was no retreat, no punting. Yes, Myles Grundler would quarterback his last contest this afternoon in his personal stadium on Paragon Drive; the flawless three-story arena, complete with swimming pool and gym that he designed and built fifteen years ago for his beloved.

The migraine subsided, and the resolute genius straightened his New York Jets cap and struggled to lift his 280-pound frame from the rigid seat. As he lumbered toward the pathway, a football one-hopped off his right knee. The former Super Bowl MVP shuffled three steps and gingerly bent over to pick up the ball.

"Over here, mister, over here," the acne-faced teenager yelled from the grassy area near an oak tree. He threw a perfect pass into the awaiting arms of the adolescent. "Thanks; nice toss, mister," the kid shouted. A feeble smile emanated from Myles' lips, as he hoisted a 'thank you' wave to the young receiver and continued his trek.

He battled the entranceway's steps and opened the front door with his key. Barb stood at the unlit fireplace perusing a magazine, her shiny black hair glistening in the sunlight. Startled, she looked up.

"What ... what are you doing here? You know you're not supposed to come here any longer. Our divorce was final. Don't you remember calling me this morning?"

Saying nothing with tears streaming down his face, the

broken man reached into his shoulder bag and withdrew the 38-Colt containing two bullets.

One shot later, glancing down at the ex-Mrs. Grundler lying dead directly in front of him, Myles' succeeding move ensured that his final game ended in a tie; just as he had orchestrated.

Prompt # 9

She loved spring.
She loved the greening of the trees, the blooms of the flowers.
She would hang the clothes outside on the line today...

The ninth prompt in this anthology highlights triggers. The idea that a moment in time can, and does, come back to us through all of our senses is not a novel idea, although it is an idea that appears in a great many novels. A well-known example is found in Marcel Proust's seven-volume *In Search of Lost Time* (also known as *Remembrance of Things Past*) which heavily relies on memories and the senses that provoke them. In the first volume, *Swann's Way*, the narrator is transported back to his childhood when he catches the scent of a particular cookie dipped in his tea.

The pieces chosen for this chapter offer a variety of pasts. The first, *Return of Spring*, hints at ancient pasts with the choices the author made for character names. The second, *Smells*, is a memoir about a time when life was simpler. The memory in the third, *Hope Springs,* is best discovered by the reader.

These are very different stories, showing again that a single prompt can be seen and used in limitless ways.

Return of Spring
Kerry E.B. Black
(617 words)

Odeletta gathered the freshly laundered bedding and headed outside. A crisp, spring breeze greeted her like a friend, and Odeletta hummed a joyful tune as she hung the sheets to dry.

A woman's voice surprised her. "Not many people hang their clothes out any more."

Odeletta laughed. "Call me old-fashioned, but I love bringing as much of the outside into my home as I can. If my bed clothes can capture a bit of this glorious scent, I'll be a happy lady."

The woman pinched her lips and nodded. "Capturing the spring has its appeal." Shadows darkened the woman's under-eyes, as though she slept poorly.

Odeletta extended a hand and introduced herself.

"Oh, you can call me Demi."

"Nice to meet you. Are you from around here?"

"I live everywhere, my dear. Today, this is my home. I'm expecting my daughter any moment now. She's been away for so long."

"That's wonderful! Was she at school?"

Demi shook her head. "Her husband locks her away, but she breaks free every spring."

"What a reason to celebrate!"

Demi nodded, her face transformed by a lush smile.

Odeletta hung the last item from the basket, wiped her hands on her back pockets, and asked, "May I offer you something to drink until your daughter arrives?"

"That would be lovely." She pointed to Odeletta's deck

furniture. "I'll wait there, if that's okay with you?"

"Wonderful idea. I'll be back in a jiffy."

Odeletta poured lemonade, plated cookies, and prepared a fruit salad of melon, grapes, and pomegranate to entertain her new friend.

"I hope you don't mind?" Demi pointed to a fire crackling in Odeletta's chimera.

"What a lovely idea. Thank you!" Odeletta set the tray on the little round table and took a seat across from her guest. Demi joined her. Warmth from the fire wrapped their picnic as they enjoyed each other's company. During their talk, Demi's eyes often slid to the hill behind Odeletta's house.

Odeletta asked, "Do you need to leave to meet your gal? I don't mean to make you late."

Demi smiled and shook her head. "She'll meet me here, if you don't mind."

Amusement worked a wide smile for Odeletta. "Do you need to phone her so that she'll know where to find you?"

"No." She leapt to her feet, joy bursting like a sun from behind troubling clouds. "Here she is! It's my Persephone!"

Odeletta turned as Demi ran to her girl. Within the indentation, of Persephone's passage, white strawberry flowers bloomed. As Demi swept her up, the plants burst forth with lush fruit. Birds serenaded overhead, and woodland creatures watched the reunion from the shadows. Odeletta felt like interloper in her own garden, enchanted, yet confused by what seemed like miraculous growth of the plants. The fire continued to comfort her, though, rendering her cozy and unwilling to leave.

Demi wrapped her arm around Persephone and guided her to the patio. She gestured. "Seph, this charming lady is Odeletta. She kept me company while I waited for you."

Persephone's voice sounded relaxing as honeybees about their work. "I'm indebted. Thank you. It is very nice to meet you." She inclined her head like a delicate swan.

The names registered. Persephone. Demeter. Could the

Greek legends walk in her garden? The lush fruits in their path would indicate so. Odeletta squinted. Did a hairy man with a hammer stand within the cave, glowering at them? Odeletta remembered her manners. "May I offer you some refreshments? You must be weary from your trip."

The hulking man turned and disappeared into the shadows, and grasses covered the entrance of the cave.

Persephone accepted a plate but laughed. "No pomegranate for me, though, please."

Smells
Deebella Clark
(472 words)

It's not the best spring day. It's not the worst spring day, but a day that I can open my window. As I do, I am immediately taken back home to Glassport, my hometown.

The smell as I opened the window was that of the foundry, where my dad worked and I can see the black lunch bucket he carried back and forth to work every day. He usually walked the many blocks it took to get to work. Sometimes he got a ride with a friend, but not often. Not a bad smell at all, but, oh, the memories that came flooding back in my mind!

I visualized so many things all at once; it doesn't seem possible that so many visions went through my head at once, but they did. I see my mom in the kitchen kneading dough to make homemade buns, the decorative glass bowl sits out, the one my mom made the salad in everyday for dinner, that bowl is in my china closet now, along with the red and white bowl my mom used in making her delicious biscuits. I treasure them. (I wonder if, when I am gone my sons will remember - I should write notes in them so they know how special they are to me, along with my baby dish when I was a baby.)

I see the produce store with Mr. Orlando sweeping out front with his hat on and Mattie walking down the main street, smiling and waving at everyone, such a sweet guy. There's Mrs. Darling from Darling's Market, and her husband and son, Saul. The dentist, Dr.Raden. Dr. Cibric, who made house calls. Dr, Finemen, the eye doctor.

I can hear the sound of the streetcar doors opening so we

could get on or off at the Paper Store. The fountain water changing colors at night. Islay's, where we got the most delicious ice cream cones and mouth watering chipped ham. I can still hear the 4 o'clock whistle signaling the end of the day shift at the foundry, and us kids knowing that it was time to head home for "supper."

We didn't have frozen food back in the day. Everything was made fresh (without antibiotics in the meat.) My mom always had a bowl of fruit for dessert on weekdays, on weekends there were pies, and cakes. I can't really remember mom making cookies except at Christmas time.

I can see the clothes hanging out to dry, towels and all, there were no dryers back then.

Yes, there is a lot in a smell, at least for me, and this I smelled when I opened the window this morning. **I love spring. I love the greening of the trees, the blooms of the flowers. I want to hang the clothes outside on the line today.**

Hope Springs
Dana Colecchia Getz
(435 words)

She loved spring. She loved that greening of the trees, the blooms of the flowers. She would hang the clothes outside on the line today and smell the crisp air of fresh beginnings.

The basket felt heavier than usual and her now large belly made it cumbersome to fit through the door. But once she maneuvered her awkward structure across the threshold and into the wooded yard, she felt a renewed sense of lightness that had left her for most of the last three months.

Her husband had encouraged her to forget about the laundry today, instead to put her swelling feet up and read a book. But, as a woman well aware of the practicality of life, she felt it best to clean the clothes today. For tomorrow, this baby might just be here and she'd simply be doing that same laundry, but with a baby to care for as well.

She leaned forward slightly to pick up a wet blouse from the pile and the baby rolled from her right side to her left. The amazement was never lost on her when she witnessed this. Stretching out through her drum tight skin she had seen her baby's foot press alien-like and felt tiny butterfly hiccups that had startled her awake. So, although she'd yet to see this little person who had somersaulted across her abdomen for these past months, she felt that they were intimate friends.

And yet, until the moment that this baby actually exits her body she knows that she will not be able to fully believe in it. Last spring the grass had also been green and the air smelled of mud and possibility, and there had been a life within her.

But as the chestnut sized baby had drained out, so had all the color of spring. Instead, there were sweaty nightmares of hollowed out and rotting abdomens, horrible glimpsing flashbacks of blood covered tile in the bathroom and her husband, desperate and terrified, calling to her on the other side of a locked door, "Are you okay? Are you okay?"

She was not. She was not sure for a long time if she ever would be again. She continued to clasp clothespin after clothespin on the line, blinking away those painful memories.

After the last pair of pants had been hung, she decided to pick some of the sunny dandelions from the knoll. They had always been her favorite flower. Spring had always been her favorite season. So much *hope.*

"I think I will go put my feet up," she thought smiling. "My baby will be here soon."

Prompt # 10

Umph, he grunted. His arm was wedged into the crevice.
For hours now, he tried to loosen it and now, surveying the sky,
he could see a big storm would soon be upon him...

Getting stuck is a common problem experienced by many writers. It is often called writer's block, but it has other names as well. Like the prompt, being stuck in writer's block is usually followed by a storm. This is not necessarily a weather related storm, but rather, a brainstorm of ideas that often happens as the result of being prompted by writing exercises or observations in life.

The three stories in this section take different paths to freeing the character in the prompt. Their endings leave the reader with very different emotions.

Fraternal Pride
Kerry E.B. Black
(548 words)

Avril stomped her foot. "This is just plain foolishness, Caleb. Just let that thing go. It's about to rain."

He adjusted his stance and pulled. With his fist balled around the object in the tree trunk, he couldn't dislodge himself, though. His forearm and shoulder muscles went from complaining to burning, but he wouldn't let the guys know of his discomfort. He stole a glance. There they were, toasting him with his brews. "Damn it. Why can't I figure this out?"

Avril glared. "You know, I thought these frat house pranks were embellished stereotypes. I believed you beyond such nonsense."

A raindrop landed like a frustrated tear on her cheek. Another colored Caleb's silk shirt.

Caleb frowned. "You don't have to stay, Avril. Go on inside and get dry."

"I'm not leaving without you."

Caleb tugged again. "Suit yourself."

The brothers rigged a kind of riddle for sophomore members, one nobody solved. Inside the hollow of the trunk they placed a sensor. They challenged sophomore brothers to remove the sensor without dropping it. The data told if the softball sized object fell. The hole in the log barely fit his fist, and once encumbered by the ball, the task proved impossible without damaging the wood, which was forbidden.

The darkened clouds unburdened themselves. Avril ran inside where the frat brothers' hoots of laughter echoed through the bog. Caleb twisted his wrist, shimmied, spun, but his hand and its burden remained stuck. As the rain fell, the ground grew marshier. The mud squelched as he tried to free his leather shoes from their suction. "Damn it." He shook his free fist at the window. "You owe me a new pair of Oxfords."

Avril returned with an umbrella. She held it over his head and toweled off his face with a cloth she retrieved from beneath her shirt. "This is so dumb, you know."

Caleb shrugged. "Yeah, you sorority sisters never do anything so thoughtless."

Avril's eyes flashed like the lightning that cut across the Louisiana sky.

"Sorry." He pulled her into a one-armed hug and pecked her cheek. The ground protested his new position with renewed sucking sounds. He looked at the umbrella. "Hope this isn't a metal rod in the middle of a lightning storm."

Avril pushed away "Yeah, I'm stupid. I brought a metal umbrella to keep us safe. Maybe I should just go."

"No, baby, don't leave." When he reached for her, he noticed the wood at the lip of the hole gave a little. She left him struggling with his dilemma. He watched as her legs beneath the umbrella carried her to the Sorority House across the quad from his home. Rain formed rivulets into his eyes and streamed down his back. He pushed his hand further into the dead tree to the thinnest place, his wrist. He cupped his opposite hand and caught rain until he could pour it over the opening of the trap. He heaved his arm with its prize, and the opening gave. He pulled again and once more until freedom.

He pumped his reddened and bruised arm with its prize toward the heavens, issuing a triumphant cry. He won the challenge. He'd make it up to Avril later, but for now, he'd bask in the adoration of his frat brothers.

E-5730
J.J. Hardic
(758 words)

E-5730 became aware of his surroundings. He was trapped in a rock formation. He tried to stand but could not. The memory files did a search on history but they were blank, then the human computer attempted a recovery of the files.

What happened? How did he get here? What was his assignment? His body sensors indicated a raise in temperature; the sun's intensity was increasing. What planet was this?

E-5730 struggled to get free but he did not have the proper leverage so he continued to lay face down on the rugged terrain. He began to retrieve certain events.

Yes.

The sun was energizing his solar receptors, and they were restoring power to him. The computer was rerouting it's systems to find a way to survive, to accomplish its mission.

Yes.

He had been through this before, several times before. The information was coming back again. He had slipped on the rocks and was trapped. The planet had a volatile weather range. He had been hit by lightning in an electrical storm, and his power went out. There were periods of darkness, then long periods of light. Similar to Earth's Alaska.

The lightning must have damaged several memory files and data banks. Now it was working to retrieve, correct, compensate, and adapt so he could complete his mission, whatever that was.

Yes.

More information was coming available. He was on this hostile planet for twenty five Earth years, stuck in the same position. Caught in a rock formation. E-5730 turned his head to assess the situation.

"Umph," he grunted. His arm was tightly wedged into the crevice. For hours now, he tried to loosen it, just like he had done the past twenty five years. E-5730 heard a rumble and surveying the sky, he could see an electrical storm would soon be upon him.

History would soon repeat itself. Lightning would strike him and knock out his electrical system. He would be off line, then darkness would fall or minimal light, not enough to reboot or affect his solar sensors. When the season of the sun would come back, he would be able to reboot to this position, only to wait for the storm.

E-5730 did an assessment of his situation and located an anomaly. He tried to free his mechanical arm and said a human term, "Umph." That was odd. He examined the other hand. A plastic polymer covered the titanium arm and hand. It too was a bit worn from the harsh weather, and there was some minute cracking and peeling. Then he thought, "What would a human do in this situation when faced with death?"

This was very odd. E-5730 had a conscious thought. Never before had he experienced this. He had no feeling but the question perplexed him. Perhaps being struck by the high voltage for twenty five years caused his computer brain to develop a new thinking pattern.

This would all be an interesting study for a later time, but the electrical storm was becoming stronger. His sensors were picking up increased ions and static electricity in the atmosphere.

E-5730 rolled to his side facing the crevice. He felt a bump when he rolled and reached down to find a laser pistol.

"Of course," he said.

For several minutes E-5730 blasted at his trapped left arm until he was able to sever it at the elbow. He retrieved it and took refuge in a nearby cave. There he listened to the crackling of the electricity and booms of the bolts hitting the nearby rocks.

The storm went on for hours, so to occupy his time E-5730 contemplated his situation while examining his mechanical arm.

"Interesting that I did a human survival strategy. How did this occur, and why did I not think about this earlier?"

He analyzed the word "thought," 'an idea produced by mental activity.' "But I have no mental activity, or do I?"

This occupied E-5730 for some time. It opened up a whole new world for him as he contemplated who he was, why was he made, and for what purpose did he serve?

E-5730's internal clock registered three days until the storm had stopped. He had done a considerable amount of thinking in that time. He emerged from the cave, set his bearings to stay along the rocks for shelter when the next storm hit. He wanted to find a human colony, perhaps they held the answers he sought.

Who was he? For what purpose was he made, and did he now have a conscience and a soul?

Blue
Dana Kerkentzes
(872 words)

Umph, he grunted. His arm was wedged into the crevice. For hours now, he tried to loosen it and now, surveying the sky, he could see a big storm would soon be upon him. *Please, God, let Blue make it home okay,* he silently prayed, *even if I don't.* The horse was surefooted and brave, braver sometimes than even he, a trait that served them well when traversing the rocky hills that lined the northern parameter of his 10,000 acre ranch. Today, though, bravery didn't much matter when a ledge broke loose beneath Blue's right hind foot, sending them plummeting into the ravine below.

He cried, not for the pain that ricocheted through his body as his arm wedged itself in that narrow fissure, but in joy as he watched his mare scramble frenziedly to her feet and gallop off in the direction of home. *She could make it back blindfolded,* he knew. *She'll be standing by the pasture gate by sunset.*

Taking comfort in this thought, he tried again to free himself, but cried out as a fresh wave of pain ripped though his body. If he didn't move, he could imagine he was laying out in the cool grass, relaxing beneath the sun after a hard day's work. But wiggle so much as a finger, and he felt like he'd fallen into the very fires of Hell. Regardless, he grit his teeth and tried again. The sound of his screams echoed through the valley.

There were stories, he knew, of hikers caught in landslides who had to chew off their own limb just to survive. He'd heard them before, read about them in the morning paper as he sipped his coffee. *But could I do it?* he wondered. *Chew off my own arm?* He shuddered at the thought.

Now, he looked again to the sky, which had finally turned

an ominous green in the hours since they had fallen. He closed his eyes and pictured Blue as she was in the first hours of her life, all wobbly legs and wonder-filled eyes as she searched for her mother's teats. When she'd had her fill of milk, he'd slipped on her first halter and carefully led them both outside. It was raining that day, just as it was beginning to rain now. Already he could hear the thunder, feel the cool mountain air as it rushed over his skin. A bolt of lightning split the sky in two. He counted, "One Mississippi, two Mississippi, three Mississippi, four, five." *Boom!* Another flash. "One Mississippi, two Mississippi, three..." The thunder moved through his body, vibrating each and every cell. With every breath he could taste the damp earth, smell his blood now mixing with rain, creating dark red eddies which swirled about him.

How much had he lost? A pint? Two? Already, he could feel the effects of shock. The world danced about him in muted greys and greens. The pounding of his heart was drowned out only by the constant barrage of rain and thunder, and now, the chattering of his teeth. He pulled his rain jacket tighter around him, thanking God he'd at least come prepared for the weather. *And praise the Lord I always wear my watch on my left arm and not the right.* He glanced at his wrist. *8:35, huh? Where are you, Blue? Did you make it home?* He sighed, wiping the rain from his face.

"Jesus Christ!" He screamed, as a bolt of lightning shot down right in front of him, leaving behind a patch of scorched earth. With his free hand, he blessed himself just as another bolt lit up the valley. It was in that brief second he could just make out the figure of what looked to be a horse laying at the bottom of the hill. *No. God, no.* He leaned forward, squinting through the rain. Yes, there it was, a horse splayed across the earth. Its legs were twisted in unnatural angles. Its head bent awkwardly towards the sky. He blinked and the vision was gone. Blinked again and it returned. The storm was receding now. A final bolt of lightning confirmed his worst fear. *No. Please, God, no.* "Blue!" He lunged forward, forgetting his captive arm for a moment and dislocating his shoulder. But there was no pain. Not anymore.

He pulled again, harder this time, desperate now to escape. "BLUE!"

He didn't notice, as he at last freed himself from the mountain, how the flesh fell away, revealing a tangle of muscle, ligament and bone. He didn't notice the sky beginning to clear as he stumbled his way down the mountainside, coming to land in a heap by Blue's side. Her eyes stared blankly at vast heavens above. Gently, he shut them with his fingertips. Then, sobbing, the man rested his head on the mare's neck and breathed in the scent of her mane. Finally, for the last time, he closed his eyes, listening for the cry of his horse's whinny and the sound of her galloping hooves come to carry him home.

A road crew in rural Alabama unearths
a papyrus scroll (intact)
when they demolish a 75 year-old culvert...

Writers frequently gather inspiration from previously written words, whether it be a list of prompts or an ancient document.

There is a special kind of magic in words. Sometimes the magic is sweet. Other times it can be gory.

The writers used opposite extremes to write the following pieces.

Note: The first story may be difficult for squeamish readers.

Ancient Scroll
J.J. Hardic
(817 words)

"What do you think Doc?" the Supervisor of the road crew asked. "As soon as we found it, I thought I'd let you guys at the University know. Do ya think it's the Dead Sea Scrolls or something?"

Professor Silverman looked through the magnifying glass studying the ancient scribbling on the paper. He gently unraveled more of the fragile paper, careful not to go too fast. He did not want it disintegrating into dust before his eyes.

"No," the Professor answered shaking his head. "No, this is something else entirely, but equally important. The Dead Sea Scrolls were found in caves around the Dead Sea, hence its name. This is quite different, some symbols I recognize, but this language is confusing with the mix of symbols for words."

"How long do ya think your team is gonna take. We need to get back on the job."

"Hopefully we can wrap this up soon. I just don't understand why this is here, in Alabama of all places."

The Supervisor rubbed his unshaven chin and left the tent the university put up. He passed one of Professor Silverman's colleagues who went into the tent.

"What do you think, Isaac?"

"You tell me, Richard. You're the linguistic expert." The man sat down opposite Professor Isaac Silverman and opened up a laptop computer.

Richard also donned the surgical gloves so he would not get any oils from his hands on the parchment. "I've cross-matched some symbols from the ancient Mayans and early native

129

Americans. It's garbled and confusing at times, some symbols have a double meaning, you can read it several different ways."

"Well, let's hear it," the Professor said. He leaned back in his field chair and pulled out a bottle of brandy and two glasses. He poured some in and drank, then filled his glass again.

"The God of Death rests here. Leave him rest. Do not allow the God of Death to rise. It will be the destroyer of man." Richard paused and sipped then continued. "Live, oh mighty one. We give you our blood, we give you our obedience, we obey, we worship you, we command you to rise and bring order to this place." Richard took another sip. "Now it goes on and on about being the destroyer of the universe and such, but its puzzling. In one way they worship this king; and, then they say they want him to stay dead."

The Professor folded his hands and looked over his reading spectacles. "Well, it's very old as you say and there can be several meanings. There could have been two distinct societies vying for power over the tribe or group. Did the students find anything, any bones, any tomb or casket?"

"No. Not yet. Interesting thought though, two distinct groups, like the Democrats and Republicans."

Professor Silverman and Richard laughed at the joke, but their laughter was cut short with cries of pain and horror. They heard the sound of heavy machinery crashing, metal against metal. They set their glasses down and heard the sound of heavy footsteps stomping in the ground. It got closer to the tent and a large shadow stood outside.

They sat frozen to their chairs hoping it was only a student playing a joke. The Professor's friend shook so much as he tried to lift his glass that the brandy spilled over its side. He used two hands and downed the remaining alcohol.

The front of the tent was torn off and an eight foot creature towered over them. It was some sort of ancient warrior. He wore a weathered and torn leather loin cloth and top which covered most of his chest, but left his huge biceps exposed. Its head was smaller and did not seem to proportionally fit its body. The skin looked gray in the light, with nicks and rips in it, like someone tried to peel it off. It had tattoo markings on its arms and chest.

Then it spoke in a foreign language. Its foul breath filled the tent, it smelled like death or some rotten type of flesh. It spoke again, this time louder and more demanding. The two doctors looked at each.

"I think ..." started Richard. "I think we brought this blasphemous thing back to life and it wants us to worship it."

"Poppycock," said Professor Silverman. He pointed his finger at his colleague. "You tell him we'll do no such thing."

Before Richard could argue the point, the grayish creature reached forward and placed its enormous hand on top of Professor Silverman's head. The Professor screamed in agony as the cracking and snapping of bones was heard.

The eight foot beast then crushed the Professor's skull as though it were an egg. Brain matter and fluid dripped from his palm. It pointed to Richard who trembled but got on his knees and bowed before the Destroyer of Civilization.

Incident
Jenifer McNamara
(454 words)

A road crew in rural Alabama unearths a papyrus scroll (intact) when they demolish a 75 year-old culvert. Robert Jones, the foreman on the job, decides to take the scroll home for safe keeping.

Upon entering his house his six year-old daughter, Lisa runs to him and asks, "What do you have there, Daddy?"

Robert puts the paperwork on the table by the door and asks, "How's my little girl doing today?" Lisa jumps into his arms and talks about how much fun she had at school. Bang!

Robert's fourteen year-old son, Derrick strides into the living room where Lisa, his sister, is sitting on their dad's lap. Derrick takes one look at them and proceeds to the stairs where he trounces and pounds on each step to the second floor where his bedroom is located Jklop!

That's the last sound Robert hears after Derrick's outrageous trek up the stairs.

"Your brother's having a bad day," says Robert.

"He's always having a bad day," says Lisa and walks into the kitchen. Robert follows Lisa and kissed Yvonne, his wife.

When silence steals away the fun, Derrick tip-toes down the stairs and sees a papyrus scroll.

He opens it. Gong! The living room is now a place with large trees, stones in a circle with ancient markings, and large black and red birds. The bright light from the moon and stars help him to see.

Derrick looks at the scroll and attempts to read it. The markings on the scroll match the markings on one large gray stone. He walks to the large gray stone and puts the scroll on the stone. In his best voice he spells out the first four words. A breeze begins to blow and clouds cover the full moon.

Derrick stops and screams, "Those clouds stole my light." He walks, finds a path, and follows it until he comes to a brook babbling ancient rhymes or reasons. He looks at the scroll and it glows. *The brook must have something to do with this scroll,* thought Derrick.

He tries to locate the words the brook is babbling on the scroll and parts of the scroll fill with underscores of red. Derrick tries to read one of the lines with red markings. Red birds fly to him and lift him off the ground. Derrick screams, "Home! Take me home!"

Someone or something understands his cries because within the next minute he's sitting on the couch in his house as if no incident ever took place. The papyrus scroll is in his hands, intact.

Robert walks into the living room, sees Derrick, and says, "Give me that. It's very important paperwork."

"Sure," says Derrick and smiles for he's glad to be home.

Prompt # 12

A sci-fi story for children:
Hello Kitty meets the Joker

This unique prompt was challenging for an odd reason. Only one person sent an entry, and that entry did not fit the "children's story" part of the prompt. Rather than face the possibility of eliminating it, the prompt was sent to some children who like to write stories. The response was delightful.

There are certain elements that define what is and what is not a children's story. Many people think that if there is a child in the story, it is for kids. That isn't always the case.

The first story in this section has a touch of science fiction, and Hello Kitty does indeed meet the Joker. However, in reality it is a story that is best suited for the adult reader, particularly one who can appreciate the cultural references and nuances. It proves that even if you don't follow the "rules" of a prompt, you can still use it as a starting point for whatever story you want to tell.

The second story is presented as it was written, including grammar and punctuation. It is included in its purest form to show that even the youngest writer can benefit from prompts. If it had been edited, the true voice of the author would be lost. She was nine when she wrote it during the summer after completing 3rd grade. The story is well thought out and engaging. It is a fun read, rich in imagery and dialogue.

Hello Kitty
J.J. Hardic
(857 words)

Hello Kitty left her house for an afternoon stroll in the park. She heard birds sing and matched the tune with a whistle. She did a little dance that matched the music, and then she broke into a Michael Jackson moonwalk and did a backward flip. She found two twigs and used them as drumsticks as she continued the song.

"Say, you're pretty good." A voice said to her.

Hello Kitty saw a man with make-up on his face sitting on a nearby bench. He looked like a clown or one those mimes that don't talk, but this one was talking.

"Why thank you. I love music, especially the classic rock of the 70's," Hello Kitty said. "What's your name?"

The man reached into the inside pocket of his red jacket and pulled out a deck of cards. With the flick of his wrist, he showed all fifty-two cards.

"They all say Joker," Hello Kitty said. "What are you doing here?"

"I'm very depressed. I've run out jokes, I don't know anymore. Everybody knows them all and nobody laughs." With the flip of his wrist, he pulled all the cards together then tossed them into a nearby garbage can. "I don't know what to do with myself. I've lost all motivation in my life."

Hello Kitty took a step back and examined the strange man with the painted face. Lipstick was at the edge of his mouth painting a smile. He wore a plaid vest with a green tie. A different shade of red pants mismatched the coat, and green and purple streaked his hair.

"I have an idea," Hello Kitty said. She went into her purse and pulled out some tissues, eye shadow, and lipstick. She cleaned the lipstick off the Joker's face and reapplied it, giving Joker a frown instead of a smile. Then she put dark eye shadow under his eyes. "There, you look like that guy, Alice Cooper. Now stand on the bench."

Joker reluctantly stood on the bench. "Now repeat this statement with power and force, like you're in a Bill Shakespeare play. Ready?"

The Joker nodded.

"Cry havoc and let slip the dogs of war."

The Joker closed his eyes and wiggled his body as if getting into character. He raised his hand to the sun and delivered the line with fire and intensity. "Cry havoc and let slip the dogs of war!"

"Perfect," Hello Kitty said in an excited tone. "How would you like to be the singer in my 70's classic rock band?"

"Really? Do you mean it? A singer in a rock band? What would we call ourselves?"

Joker jumped off the bench and sat down. They started to throw out names. "The Hello Kitty Band, Joker and the Wild Cards, White Sunday, Shallow Blue, Red Manhattan Clam Chowder Cult, The Standing Boulders, The June Bugs and several others before settling in on Joker and the Wild Cards.

"Our message will be one of hope and striving to reach your goal in life, no matter what it is, or how difficult the odds are," Hello Kitty said. "We can take some classic songs from groups and rename them as well as the words like that weirdo Al or Tom or whatever his name is."

The Joker jumped with glee as Hello Kitty called several other friends to put the band together. That night they started like every other 70's band and played in Hello Kitty's garage.

Soon a large crowd gathered and cheered until they heard the siren of a police car.

"Alright now," the policeman said. "It's time to break this

up."

"Hey wait a minute." Hello Kitty said. "We can use that in one of our songs."

"You can?" The policeman said.

"Yes. The Joker and I really liked the way you said 'alright now.' That was great. It can be the start of an anti-war song."

"Or a pro-war song." The Joker chimed in and then laughed. "Start the siren again if you don't mind Officer.....Ozzy."

Soon the band was playing the small club circuit, then the local colleges. The students loved the music and they were booked on an American College Tour and found themselves the opening act for major bands.

Everybody wanted to see Joker and the Wild Cards, singing 70's classic songs with their twist, songs like "Twenty First Century Bipolar Man," "I Love Myself Narcissistically," "Purple Battleship," "Smoke Over the H2O," and the audience's favorite, "Fatzilla."

At the end of every show, the Joker always thanked the fans and said how grateful he was to them. He realized that, without fans buying their music and coming to see them play, he would still be sitting on a park bench.

"And finally I would like to say that sometimes things may not make sense to you at that moment, but there is a reason. Have faith. Have faith in yourself and that in time you'll understand. If I didn't go to that park on that specific day, and hadn't sat on that specific spot, then I would have missed Hello Kitty and all this would never have happened."

Hello Kitty Meets the Joker
Isabella Sanchez
(Age 9)
(478 words)

Once upon a time, Hello Kitty was looking on her phone. She thought, "Hey, there is a carnival tomorrow! I think I'll go."

The next day, when she got to the carnival, she saw so many rides! First, she went on the bumper cars. (That was her favorite ride.) When she got into line, she saw that there were only two or three people in the line.

She thought, "Hey! Why are there so many people on the other rides, but there aren't any people on this ride?! Only three people!"

But, she went on the ride anyway. When she got on the ride, it started out slowly. You could go only four miles an hour, but then you couldn't move your car at all! Hello Kitty looked up at the controls for the ride and she saw that the Joker was controlling the ride!!!

She jumped out of her bumper car, and right after she did they went crazy!!! They were going 20 miles an hour! And then...they CRASHED!!! (No one got hurt but the bumper cars were all banged up.)

The Joker ran off, but Hello Kitty ran after him. He was so fast that she had a hard time keeping up with him. He was sneaky, too. He tried to hide from her by going behind the rides.

First, they went into the bouncy house. Hello Kitty had a hard time catching him because he was so fast. After the bouncy house, they went in the hall of mirrors. Hello Kitty got really tired because the Joker was really fast. So, Hello Kitty started to go a little slower because she was very tired. The Joker got away.

She stopped to catch her breath, and saw millions of Jokers! (Because the mirrors make things seem like the real thing that's in front of it is in the mirrors). Hello Kitty was so confused! She tried to grab him, but all she caught was a mirror. This happened over and over again.

Then finally, she knew which one was the real Joker. She raced towards him. He screamed and ran away. Then he jumped on a ride that was the like the Dumbo ride, but it was a squid theme. Hello Kitty jumped on, too. Round and round they went until finally the Joker jumped off.

When she finally caught him the cops came, and he went to jail for a very long time.

THE END

Wait! That wasn't the end of the story!

Hello Kitty came to jail to visit the Joker. She said, "I brought him cakes that didn't have escape plans or things that would help him escape because I felt bad for him."

Two years later the Joker escaped from jail. Was Hello Kitty really telling the truth about the cakes? Or, did the Joker escape a different way?

THE REAL END

Prompt # 13

Happy Birthday – Thomas Jefferson.
What do you do when you find him wandering
through your CURRENT neighborhood?

The first of the two stories that were selected for this prompt has a touch of mystery, suspense, and a hint of supernatural. The author has a gift for leading the reader in one direction, and delivering them a reveal that brings either a gasp of horror or a sigh of relief. In this piece the twist takes a different path.

The second story touches on a reality that is all too familiar to many people. While the subject the author chose to use may be painful to some, he delivers a delightful look into a world that many will face at some point.

Both stories will leave the reader with unanswered questions.

What is reality? What is fantasy? What is delusion?

Quill of Destiny
Kerry E.B. Black
(675 words)

Abby's footfalls splashed a percussion of discontent as she thundered through her neighborhood. Thick fog rolled from the river, stealing through the alleyways around her, but she paid it no mind. She inhaled deep, trying to calm herself with exertion. She clutched her latest rejection letter in her fist, its scathing remarks causing her heart to pump doubt through her scribbler veins. "Couldn't get past the third paragraph, indeed," she mumbled.

The pathway ascended a steep hill, and by its apex, she gasped for breath. She bent at the waist, hands on her knees, to steady her breathing. Strange music drifted with the breezes. Fife and drum? She smoothed the bone-white paper in her hand and squinted at its words beneath the streetlamp. "Conseder another line of work," wrote the editor. Abby snorted at the typographical error. "Great editing on that rejection letter, dumb butt," she thought. "Here's what I think of your assessment of my work," she said, ripping the page into confetti and throwing it into the air. It floated to the sidewalk like a tickertape parade passed.

She hummed "Yankee Doodle" as she continued home. As she rounded the final corner, she heard male voices raised in heated discussion. Probably politics. Election years effected everyone, after all. She walked up her driveway, passed the front porch, and stopped before opening the back door to the kitchen. Lights blazed inside.

She reached into her jacket pocket and dialed the police. "I think someone broke into my house. She gave her address and was instructed to wait for the officers' arrival. "I don't even know if anyone is in there," she complained. Patience was advised, but instead, Abby pulled out her canister of compressed mace and peeked inside.

A man sat at her kitchen table, his back to her. His folded hands rested before him. She didn't recognize him.

Minute followed minute. The man sat statue-still. No police arrived. Abby tapped the plastic mace cylinder, considering.

She burst through the kitchen door, wielding the mace before her. She rounded on the stranger, retrieving a cast iron skillet along the way.

Something about the man, dressed as a reenactor of some sort, seemed familiar. Her arm wearied as she held the pan before her. "Who are you, and why are you in my kitchen?"

The man stood and bowed from his waist. "We've been waiting for you, Ms. Abigail. We are the Spirit of '76, and we require your assistance."

The pan shook from the strain of suspending it before her. "I beg your pardon?"

"No, my dear lady, it is we who beg your pardon. It must be a terrible surprise to find a stranger thrust upon you in the dead of night. I assure you we wouldn't have come unless the need were vital."

She searched the room. "We? Are there more of you here? Where are they hiding?"

"Only one of us can speak at a time. It is the way of things. Please sit."

She slid into a spot at the head of the table where she could see him. Angular nose. Intelligent eyes. Hair pulled into a cue at the base of the high collar of his neck. "Are you," she hesitated at the absurdity, "Are you supposed to be Thomas Jefferson."

A smile played at the corners of his mouth as he nodded. "We've noticed your prose and are impressed."

She stifled a giggle. Thomas Jefferson admired her writing. Take that, stupid rejection letter!

"We have need of your eloquence."

"Wouldn't it be better to ask someone who, you know, has something besides a couple of poems published?"

"We agreed you will do well. We have faith in you, and your country needs you."

"But, I don't know much about politics."

"We'll help you there, too," he said.

From the shadows, a man presented a quill and parchment with a flourish. "Thank you, Hancock," Thomas Jefferson said. "We'll help you with the ideas, but you must write the words."

She accepted the quill and with it, her destiny.

A Simple Solution
Bill McKinley
(273 words)

"You better get those taxes done, Mil. You've only got two more days after today, you know."

"Okay, okay. I'm working on them; so quit bugging me about it, already. If I don't get them done today, I'll finish them tomorrow. Oh, shit. There's Thomas Jefferson walking out there in my garden. Why does he do that every year on his birthday? Oh, well, there goes another day to not work on the taxes. I guess I'll finish them on the fifteenth."

"The hell with Thomas Jefferson. Let somebody else worry about him this year. Finish those taxes."

"Don't sweat the small stuff, Abigail. I'll handle this. It's a simple solution."

Millard exits the back door and approaches Thomas.

"Hey, Tom. How about I give you some of my wife's freshly baked cupcakes, cookies, and an apple pie to take back to share with your friends tonight? Okay?"

Mr. Jefferson accedes to the homeowner's wishes and gets into the car.

After a short drive, Ms. Hemings greets them at the door.

"Oh, Thomas, you've returned. I was so worried about you," Sally says.

"Are Mr. Jefferson's buddies around? He's got some pastries to share with them," Millard asks.

"Oh yes, they are in the recreation area. Follow me."

They enter the large room and Thomas' friend clears her throat.

"Attention: Messrs. Washington, Adams, Lincoln, DaVinci, Shakespeare, Sinatra, Einstein: Mr. Jefferson has returned, and he brought goodies for your Poker game, tonight."

Washington and Adams straighten their wigs, and the motley crew rushes to greet Thomas.

"Thank you, Ma'am," Mr. Fillmore replies, as he descends the front steps of the Miami Memory Loss Manor.

Prompt # 14

Reinaldo held her in his muscled arms, nuzzling her neck.
His hand slid down her back.
She froze in his arms.
"Reinaldo," she cried, "please...."

The authors who wrote the chosen pieces in this section usually write fantasy, horror, and science fiction. The stories they wrote for this prompt do not fit these genres in an obvious way. This exercise prompted both authors to stretch their imaginations and try different writing styles. This use of prompts is one of the very best. When experimenting with new genres, it doesn't really matter if the resulting stories are potential prize winners or not. What does matter is that the author was willing to reach outside of their comfort zone. Sometimes doing this can result in a love for a new writing style. Other times a hidden talent for an unexpected type of story or poetry.

These sample stories also reflect the very unique way each writer sees a prompt. In one story Reinaldo's potential lover invites him to continue. In the other, she pleads with him to stop. One story changed the spelling of Reinaldo to Renaldo. That does not matter at all. It was still a valid use of the prompt. Remember, prompts can be utilized in any way the writer wishes.

Reinaldo's Frustration
Kerry E.B. Black
(632 words)

Araceli recoiled from Reinaldo, head drooping and shoulders hunching over like a melting statue. "Please, no." Tears dangled on the ends of her over-long lashes as though hesitant to leave her eyes.

He nestled close again, pleading, "Come on, Araceli. Just a little kiss."

She crossed her arms and turned away.

He pitched a cigarette butt to the ground at her feet. Its smoke stretched a sensual dance up her skirt and hugged her legs. He licked sweat from his lips, enjoying the salt. "Nobody else would put up with your crap. You know that, right?"

Araceli blinked wide eyes from behind a curtain of bangs.

His heart quickened. With a finger, he lifted her drooping chin. "You're so beautiful," he thought, but he said, "Boyfriends and girlfriends hug. They kiss. They hold hands. Heck, I've even heard of the occasion when a guy and a girl in love might, you know..."

She bit her trembling lip.

He longed to crush her to his chest and cover her lips with his. "What are you so afraid of? I mean, you've known me since we were kids." He remembered her trembling in the doorway, clutching a backpack to her chest. She wouldn't talk for years, just sat at her desk a silent and often forgotten observer. The classroom rumor pegged her as a charity case, a foster whose family abandoned their stupid girl. She failed tests and ignored the teachers. Instead, she waltzed through the halls, head tilted toward the window as though listening to songs on the breezes.

One time, when a teacher asked him to deliver a note to the teacher's lounge, Reinaldo overheard the adults discussing her. They had used word like "trauma" and "learning disability." It had hurt Reinaldo to imagine Araceli's struggles. He watched her from the corners of his observations, and when Araceli required a tutor, Reinaldo volunteered on the sly. When his classmates teased, he shrugged and blamed the teacher. Privately, he loved every moment of time with her and relished trying to break through to her.

A gust of wind blew her long hair across her face. When it calmed, he brushed a tendril behind her ear.

She stepped away from his reach.

He threw his hands into the air. "Serves me right. I'm always taking in strays. Drives my mom crazy." He flushed at his rudeness. Instead of apologizing, he flashed a frustrated smile and sidelong glance. "Do you know, I have two dogs, three cats, a turtle, and a guinea pig? All rescued." He bumped her side with an elbow. "See, I'm a good guy."

A timid smile stretched her lips, and on impulse, he swept her in a hug. She smelled of spring air and felt warm and soft in all the right places. The earth seemed to spin. He closed his eyes, imagining they fell through clouds together. "Oh, man," he breathed into her ear. He stretched his fingers along her back, inching one hand up and the other down.

With a strangled cry, she pushed against his chest. "No!"

He stepped back, short of breath. Confusion vied with anger and hurt for dominance.

She ran the path through the blooming gardens, her hair streaming behind her like stratus clouds. His stomach clenched, and he ached to run after her, to bring her back, to tell her he loved her. His hands remembered the feel of her. Smooth, tight skin, a soft derriere, but something strange along her shoulder blades. A row of knots, hard as bone, provide a rocky landscape where there should have been smooth peaks and valleys of shoulders and spine.

As she disappeared around the corner, he decided to try to understand, to be patient, and to win her heart no matter how long she needed.

Romantic Evening, Almost
J.J. Hardic
(617 words)

Renaldo held her in his muscled arms, nuzzling her neck. His hand slid down her back. She froze in his arms, "Renaldo," she cried, "please, take me."

Renaldo kissed her neck, then her shoulder moving her blouse as far as it would go, then he stopped. He took a step away, turned and left the room. Sarah leaned against the wall taking deep breaths waiting with anticipation.

"Where did he go?" she asked herself.

Renaldo returned with his shirt back on as well as a light brown suit jacket which matched his shoulder length hair. He had keys in his hands.

"Where do you want to go?"

"What?"

"Where do you want me to take you?"

Sarah gave him a perplexed look. This couldn't be happening. She was expecting a romantic evening with a good looking hunk that was as dumb as dirt. Renaldo stood there jiggling the keys to his car.

"I will take you where ever you want to go."

All the passion left Sarah. She straightened up against the wall and fixed her blouse. "I thought we'd just go back down to the hotel bar and have a few drinks, maybe an appetizer platter. It's still early."

After a few drinks, Sarah realized that this hunk was no Einstein. He looked at himself in any reflective surface he could. He touched his hair every few seconds putting some fallen strand back in place. And aside from being narcissistic, he thought himself a wonderful gift to woman.

He knew nothing of world affairs or even current events, but he could deliver a line that worked in some movie.

"You have lovely eyes. I have never seen lips as perfect as yours. You are a very attractive woman. I have not met someone as beautiful, and as charming as you in a long time."

Yeah, yeah, yeah. And the flattery went on and on and on until she asked him up to her room. What the heck was she thinking?

Now Sarah was angry at herself for falling for all of that crap and with a guy that wanted to be on the cover of some historical romance novel.

Now all she wanted was to get rid of him.

She felt like she was babysitting some thirty year old going on thirteen. Well a thirteen year old would be more mature, and he would probably carry on a better conversation.

Renaldo or Fabio or whatever his name was examined his manicured nails, and then he took his hand and ran it alongside his head to put a misplaced hair strand back in its proper place. He looked at his watch then leaned forward over the table. He placed his hand on hers.

"You know Sarah. I love the smell of your hair. The way you wear it only compliments your beauty, especially your eyes. You have lovely eyes. Tonight, I hope we can make love all night long, until the sun comes up. Then I will take you for a lovely drive for breakfast and then we can make love again."

That was all that Sarah could handle.

"Renaldo, you're such a nice young man, but I am sorry to disappoint you. Suddenly I am very tired and not in the mood to make love, especially since eating all this food. It's giving me indigestion." She broke her hand free from his grasp. "Oh, look at the time. I have to go take my medicine so the voices don't come back."

Sarah left the table leaving Renaldo wondering what she meant by taking medicine so that she would not hear voices.

"Well that was a romantic evening, almost." Sarah said as she pushed the elevator button.

Prompt # 15

Taxes – you find out that you are
mistakenly given a refund for a million dollars,
but the IRS refuses to believe you that it's a mistake.
What do you do?

One of the most famous quotations by Benjamin Franklin is "Nothing is certain except death and taxes." It is sometimes quoted as "Nothing is certain but death and taxes." Whichever way he stated it, the great truth of his age remains true today. What can change is the way people may relate to the statement. It is generally supposed that "taxes" refer to the money citizens pay to the government for services. This type of taxes can lead to "taxing" situations of frustration, confusion, and anxiety. As for death, while it usually is considered the end of life, it may also mean the end of relationships, hopes and dreams.

The three stories in this section flow through levels of anxiety, confusion, and frustration before landing in each of the above named types of death. The characters are unique and range from sweet to strong to sassy. The third story alludes to a classic comedy routine with amusing results.

Death and Taxes
Kerry E.B. Black
(352 words)

The diagnosis stood. Three doctors agreed. Inoperable. Terminal.

Spring held no appeal. Shelagh did not feel the flower-scented breezes. She paid no mind to the children playing in the park. She replayed the medical jargon and marched through her neighborhood, angry. She followed the rules of good health. She ate right and exercised. No smoking, and only an occasional glass of wine passed her lips. Doctors predicted within a year, forty-four-year-old Shelagh would die.

She passed an old couple. He had his arm around her osteoporosis-ridden body. Shelagh had never married. A young woman pushed a pram ahead. Shelagh never bore children. She never traveled as she intended. She worked for a small paycheck, lived in a shabby apartment, and enjoyed little of her existence.

Her breath burned in her chest as she collected her mail. Bills, a circular, and a letter from the IRS. She collapsed into the sofa, avoiding its protruding spring, and ripped open the letter.

"Dear Ms. Shelagh O'Brady, Your tax refund has been deposited into your account..."

Shelagh sat up, certain her eyesight must be going. "...the amount of one million dollars and sixty-seven cents..." She rubbed her eyes and read again. Same number.

She dialed the government number listed at the top of the letter. When she reached an agent, she explained, "There is a mistake."

"We see no mistake, Ms. O'Brady."

"No, really, I don't think I've earned a million dollars in my entire lifetime, let alone earned enough to be issued such a refund."

The sound of typing proceeded the same, dispassionate response. A supervisor could find no error, either.

Shelagh hung up, baffled. Her stomach twisted, and shooting pain sent her curling into the couch cushions. When it passed, she pulled herself to unsteady legs. She surveyed her home. Thrift-shop furniture. Damaged television. Leaking appliances. She sighed, speaking to the loneliness. "What a way to live."

The letter from the IRS rested atop the errant couch spring like a royal proclamation. Instead of a gown, perhaps Shelagh's fairy godmother waved a magic wand. Instead of a ball, the edict was clear. "Live, Cinderella."

One for the Money
Louise Eckman
(867 words)

I closed the door as I left the local IRS office; our meeting had ended. My heart pounded. The IRS representative told me I was authorized to cash the check they had sent me for $1,089,482.00. I had insisted I was not entitled to that refund. The rep had smiled and said, "Oh yes you are!" So the truth was out - I had become a millionaire.

My first thought - to talk to someone in my circle of family and friends. However, by the time I reached my parking lot, I realized I had better postpone that. I had read an article online about how people who win lotteries were pressured by family and friends for money.

It was only four o'clock, but the sun had dropped behind the building where I lived, casting a long shadow over the lot. I slowly headed upstairs to my apartment, wondering if my boyfriend would be home. We had lived together almost a year and the relationship had descended into constant bickering. "Don't tell him about the money," I told myself firmly.

"Hi, Jamie," I said as I saw him sitting in front of the TV. There was no response.

"I should leave this guy," I said to myself, "I can afford to do anything I want."

"Hey, Jamie," I said louder, "I'm talking to you!"

"Hi, Honey," he murmured without turning his face away from the TV.

Putting my coat and purse in the closet, I wandered into the kitchen to look for dinner.

"Hey, Bella," Jamie said and turned toward me, "did you

see that guy at the IRS today?"

"Yeah, I saw him. I met with him downtown at the IRS office. Everything is good and the whole $1089 dollars is mine!"

"Great," he responded. "Let's go out to dinner and celebrate."

"Uh oh," I thought to myself. *This is exactly what I was afraid of - he is going to spend my money.* This is why I lied to him, telling him it was $1089 and not $1,089,482.00 that I had received.

"Great idea, Jamie," I said. Then I turned to the closet to choose an outfit for the evening. Jamie and I dressed in better clothing that we wore to work that day. Then he hugged me and said, "This is great, Bella. I am a new fan of the IRS. Where'll we go to eat?"

As we descended the stairs to the parking lot, we considered a few places to eat and chose one. Our time in the restaurant started out pleasantly. We ordered a bottle of champagne and toasted the IRS. Jamie scrolled through his messages on his phone.

"I met with Carlos' mom at lunch today," I told Jamie. Carlos was a seven-year-old in my class who was struggling with reading. Jamie slowly shifted his gaze from his phone to my face. He said nothing. So I continued to describe my meeting with the mother. Gloom invaded my head when I realized how little we actually talked.

That evening we cuddled up in front of the TV and watched the news. A few minutes into it, we started to slowly rub each other. That quickly morphed into foreplay and we made love on the sofa.

Later, while trying to fall asleep, I was thinking about our lack of communication. Then I began to worry about the IRS lie and how to handle it. I wondered if he would want to go out to dinner every night, and what else might he want to do with my money?

At 6 a.m. the alarm clock rang and I woke up feeling

groggy. I had hardly slept at all. Jamie was sound asleep as usual, and snoring lightly. Suddenly, I realized - I don't need to go to work ever again!

But my work was my life. I loved teaching, even though it was a lot of hard work. Puzzled and alarmed, I put on my bathrobe and walked into the kitchen. Looking out the window above the sink, I saw large snowflakes coming down. There were several inches of snow on top of my car. "Maybe this will become a school delay and give me some time to get my thoughts together."

I went to my laptop and Googled "financial advice". An article about lottery winnings emphasized personal security. They suggested getting an advisor to help you manage your winnings before discussing the winnings with friends and family. I felt relieved and pleased with myself. I had not mentioned the actual amount of the IRS refund to anyone yet – mostly because I didn't think it would happen!

One click on the local TV station's site told me "Longwood School District Closed Today".

"Hooray!" I thought and suddenly imagined myself collecting a bunch of boxes, packing up and moving out. In an hour or so, Jamie would be going to work. Eight hours would be enough time for me to pack my belongings and find a place to stay. Dressing quickly and quietly, I went down to the parking lot. I swept the snow from my windshield and then started the car. I headed to the grocery store to look for boxes.

Taxes
J.J. Hardic
(870 words)

"This can't be right," Joe said. "Someone definitely missed a decimal point." Joe put the refund check from the Internal Revenue Service on his desk and dialed the number. He got the robot recording instructing him which numbers to push.

Each time the recording thanked him for calling the IRS and directed him to another number to push. Finally he reached the correct department.

"There are callers ahead of you," the recording said. "Your current wait time is two hours."

Joe put the intercom on his phone on and listened to the elevator music. He went on the computer and searched his social media sites to pass the time. Every so often the music would stop, and the recording would say how much time he had to wait. When it got down to less than fifteen minutes, Joe closed his laptop and waited for someone to answer.

"Thank you for calling the Internal Revenue Service," the voice said.

"Hello, my name is Joseph Dalusha and I just received my refund check."

"All our offices are closed for the day. Please call back between the hours of nine and five. Your call is important to us and we want to help you as best we can."

Joe was furious and clicked off the phone. He went online but due to an overflow of people, Joe was unable to log onto the web site.

The next day Joe decided to work from home and placed a call at five after nine to the IRS. He again went through all the buttons and departments until he got the two hour recording message. He did paperwork and patiently waited for the next available agent.

"Hello, this is agent Randal Rothmen. How can I assist you?"

"Oh great. My name is Joseph Dalusha and there was a mistake on my refund check."

"Alright sir. I need some basic information and we'll get things straightened out."

Randal typed in the computer Joe's social security number and address and pulled up his file. "Alright sir, what seems to be the problem?"

"It's the million dollar refund. It's a mistake."

"Sir. The IRS does not make mistakes."

"Somebody placed the decimal point in the wrong place. I should only get a thousand dollars."

"Sir, even if the decimal point was misplaced, then that would make it ten thousand dollars. That cannot be the case. Unless you're saying that you should be getting one hundred million dollars, which isn't going to happen in a million years."

"No. I'm not saying that at all."

"Then what are you saying?"

"I'm saying that I'm not supposed to be getting one million dollars."

"You are Joseph Dalusha correct?"

"Yes."

"It says here you got a check for a refund of one million dollars, correct?"

"Yes."

"Well sir, then I fail to see what the problem is."

"Oh my stars in heaven." Joe said to the agent. "I feel like I'm in Abbott and Costello's who's on first routine."

"Who's on first?" Randal asked.

"I don't know, third base?"

"Sir. Did you file on behalf of Mr. Abbott and Mr.

Costello?"

"No."

"Is it one person, Abbott N. Costello? What is the middle name?"

"No. It's not like that at all."

"Sir. I am trying to help you as best I can. You are going to have to be more clear and precise. Now who are you filing in behalf of?"

"Myself. Joseph Dalusha."

"Then why are you giving me Mr. Abbot N. Costello's name? Is this the name of your business? What type of business is this?"

"No. Wait, what?"

"Sir. I'm sorry but I'm going to have to direct you to my supervisor."

Joseph heard a click and the elevator music came back on. He rubbed his eyes and ran his fingers through his hair. He massaged his temples as he looked at his watch to see how much time passed. After five minutes another voice came on.

"Hello, Mr. Costello? My name is Barb Bolaski. How can I help you?"

"My name is Joe. Joseph Dalusha."

"Is Mr. Costello there with you?"

"No."

"How about Mr. Abbott?"

"No. There is no Abbott or Costello." Joe was now getting irritated and testy.

"Mr. Dalusha. There is no reason to get angry. We are trying to help here. That is our motto. If there is no Abbott and Costello, then why did you bring them into the scenario?"

"I was making a joke."

"Misrepresenting yourself to the IRS is no joke Mr. Dalusha. Neither is filing a fraudulent claim. We take our work here seriously."

"Oh, dear God." Joe said in an exasperated tone.

"There is no reason to invoke God here either. We practice separation of Church and State. In fact, we are God here.

"Now, let's talk about these million dollars you owe us and how you are going to pay it back."

"How about if I write you a check? It will be in the mail tomorrow."

"Now was that so difficult Mr. Dalusha?"

"No Ma'am. Thank you." Joseph shook his head and hung up the phone. "Why did I even bother to try to explain a mistake to a government agency?"

Prompt # 16

Saturday, in the park...
but YOU think it's the 4th of July...

There are times when chaos and confusion steal the spotlight. This is the case for the second story in this section. When work becomes overwhelming, people often seek refuge in a relaxing environment like a park. One such person discovers that there are worse things than an overbearing boss and better ways to live life than trying to escape reality.

The first story emphasizes what can happen if typical social time concepts (such as days, dates, and calendars) are ignored. Almost everyone has lost track of the day or date at some point in their life, but few can survive by ignoring time completely. The author of this piece takes a peek into the life of one such person. Discover what happens to this memorable character.

A Case for Calendars
Hana Haatainen-Caye
(970 words)

I ain't never been fond of calendars. Or dates. A Sunday is a Monday is a Tuesday. They're all the same. Christmas, Thanksgiving, Columbus Day. I only 'spect it's a holiday when the mailman fails to stuff the box and even then, sometimes I wonder if it's just a Sunday.

I work from home – freelancing, you know. Graphics. And I pay no attention to due *dates*. I give hours, not dates, for deadlines. "I'll have this to you in 48 hours," I promise, and I *always* deliver on that promise. That's smart business, don't ya think?

So, this one hot summer day, I'm eating a bagel at Daisy's Coffee, Tea and Ghee and I overhear some girls giggling over their plans for Saturday. They were slobberin' over meetin' some guy in the park. Why do girls act that way? I'll never figure it out. But then I heard them mention the Fourth of July. On Saturday. Apparently, that was only three days away.

Chicago played on the coffee shop oldies station. "Saturday in the park; I think it was the Fourth of July." And just like that, a memory popped into my mind. A memory of a promise I made some twenty-odd years ago.

"Meet me in the park every year that the Fourth of July falls on a Saturday," she'd said. I guess I was a slobbery kind of a guy back then and she's the one who made me slobber.

"It's a date," I'd said.

"No matter what, okay?" She said it don't matter if we were married to someone else or what. Even if we had a whole slew of kids, we'd still keep that date. "Just keep it a secret. Your wife

164

won't have to know."

Yep, just like that, I promised my Fourth of July Saturdays to Ellie. A few years later, I threw out my calendars and forgot about it.

I semi-choked on my bagel, wondering how many times I'd let her down. It's been oh, I don't know, twenty years or so since then. Surely she's not still waiting there under that ol' weeping willer tree by the crick. But just 'cause I didn't keep the promise don't mean she didn't. Crap.

Seventy-two hours. I had to know. I had to go.

* * *

It was Saturday morning. I knew 'cause I'd counted the hours. I even counted 'em in my sleep. Not that I slept. Not really. I just kept thinkin' 'bout Ellie, wondering if she still had those chinchilla-soft fingers. She'd touch me and I could barely feel it. Yet the darndest thing of it was I could feel it everywhere. She'd brush them fingers of hers over my forearm and I'd feel it 'cross my spine. Then I'd get them doggone goose pimples and she'd giggle. That's when I'd start that ol' slobberin'. No wonder I couldn't sleep. Hadn't thought of Ellie for years.

I stopped at Daisy's for a cup o' Joe to fortify me. Wanted a Jack, but it was too early in the day for that. Then I headed 'cross town to the park. It was only three-and-a-half miles away from my trailer, but I hadn't been there in years. I used to go sit by that tree, pretending to fish, in the fall after she left for university. God I missed her back then. Me? I stayed in town and went to the local community college. But it was good. It was enough. I got my associate's in graphic art and I've done okay with it. Like I said, I don't hafta punch a clock like my brothers – both of 'em corporate big shots. Big shots, my ass. Tied to them damn calendars. Appointments, you know? And mortgages that keep 'em working every hour of every day.

I drove into the park, my tires spitting stones outta the way. It was surprisingly empty for a holiday. I expected lots of family picnics and kids playing on the swing sets and slides. Maybe it was just too early. I crossed the grass, relieved to see my old friend, the willer, still spreading its leafy branches over the crick. Ellie wasn't there, but like I said, it was early. I'd sit and I'd wait, just like I imagined she'd done many times since 1992. Damn. How could I forget?

I sat down on the bank of the crick and watched the minnows swarm. "You didn't forget, you dumb ass," I said to myself. It was true. I remembered. At least that first time. Fact is, I was ashamed. I'd heard she was workin' on some fancy doctorate degree. Compared to her, I was just a bum livin' in a trailer without a so-called "real" job. I intentionally "forgot" to show up. And eventually, forgettin' came naturally.

But not this year.

By one o'clock, I was hot, tired, and thirsty. Plus, I had to piss. I stood up and stretched and walked off in search of a porta john. I spotted the gigglin' girls from Daisy's sitting on a picnic table. No sign of the boy they'd been slobberin' over. I kept walkin'.

Then I saw it – a big red, white, and blue sign posted on a pole next to the johns.

Independence Day Celebration
Friday, July 4, 2014
Noon to 11:00 p.m.

Friday? I'd missed it. That's why no one was around. The Fourth of July was on Friday, not Saturday. Damn. "Damn," I said out loud. "Damn. Damn. Damn." I yanked open the green door, stepped inside, and took a piss. "Damn," I said as I stepped back out onto the grass, pullin' up my fly as I did.

Then I walked 'cross the parking lot, got in my truck, and drove over to Buck's Bar and Grill. It was time for that Jack after all.

Saturday in the Park
J.J. Hardic
(701 words)

Saturday, in the park...but you think it's the 4th of July. People were laughing, people were jogging, a man was selling ice cream, and a clown was giving balloons to children.

Carlos sat on a park bench watching this play out. Spring in the park. The cherry blossoms were coming out and some teenagers on skateboards whizzed by. They were playing some sort of game, and one of them pulled out a gun and aimed it at the other. They laughed and shot paint balls at each other. A red splatter hit a tree; another orange one caught a trash can, making a large thud.

"Idiots!" Carlos said to anyone who would listen.

The park resumed its springtime atmosphere. Carlos looked at the messages on his phone. His boss was looking for him and wanted to meet. Carlos rubbed his eyes as prices, productivity, and percentages ran through his mind. Did they meet their quota this month, or this week? How much did they make or not make? Who was highest, which team came in first and last? Would he have to endure yet another chewing out, or worse, another speech by the manager that there was dead weight on the team? Not everyone was pulling in their quota and heads just might have to roll.

Then all hell broke loose.

A young woman ran past him pushing a baby carriage and yelled at Carlos to run. A man ran by carrying a child in his arms.

"Get out of here quick! They're coming!"

Before Carlos could ask what was going on, a large white Siberian tiger jumped over his bench, turned and looked at him in the eyes. It growled and snarled at him, showing its teeth. The tiger raised its paw, showing the long claws ready to swipe him. It sniffed the air and roared, ready to pounce.

In that short time span, Carlos reviewed his life. What he had done, what he had accomplished. How heartbroken his family would be hearing of his death.

But where did these cats come from? The zoo? How did they break out?

Carlos thought of how fate intervened that day. Of all the days he decided to come to the park for a lunch break, it was now. He had chosen this specific seat, this specific bench, at this specific time. And now, he would soon meet his maker.

Carlos heard the large cat roar, as if daring him to move or strike; and then he heard another roar behind the tiger. It was a second Siberian tiger.

The one in front turned as if to respond, and Carlos saw what it was that so angered the beasts. The one had red paint markings on its side. The other had an orange marking on its head and a red one on its side.

The first beast turned and roared back to the second, and then they speed off as if they caught the scent of food.

Carlos sat for a quiet moment, relieved that he escaped the cats' jaws. He breathed deeply and watched his hand shake for a while. He tried to stand, but his legs were wobbly and rubbery so he sat back down. He picked up his phone and started to dial but stopped when he heard the shrieks and screams of two men in agony.

The Siberian tigers found who they were looking for.

Carlos finished dialing 911 and reported what was happening to the police. Then he called his work and informed them that he would be late coming back to work.

"He keeps walking by your cubicle to see if you're there," the secretary on the other end said.

"Well. He has a surprise waiting for him when I do get back Margie. I have a new perspective on things."

He dialed a number and let it ring until he heard a voice.

"Hey Mom, it's me. I was just sitting here in the park and I thought I'd give you a call. Listen, I have to get back to work, but I'm going to take some time off and come home to visit. Tell Dad to look at the baseball schedule and pick a game."

Prompt # 17

Another day...in the park...
Every day IS the 4th of July.
What happens in your world?

If every day was July 4th, or Christmas, or your birthday, it would no longer be unique or special. There have been books and movies made to examine what life would be like if every day was the same as every other day. Two examples that some readers may be familiar with are *Elmo Saves Christmas* and *Groundhog Day*. In both cases, the characters are forced to relive a day that was once special to the main characters, but by their repetition become not only unimportant, but also annoying and exasperating.

Both authors of the following stories keep the reader in suspense, and lead them to want to know more. By the end of the stories the reader is left to wonder what would happen if a similar thing would happen in their own world.

Yet Another Day
J.J. Hardic
(640 words)

Roger sat up and coughed. The ground was still wet from the morning dew. The sun broke through the trees, and he heard the sounds of birds and people on the trails. He pulled all his belongings together and grabbed a towel he had taken from the homeless shelter days before.

Roger went into a nearby restroom and washed his face. He returned to his spot and waited. A young couple came by walking with their coffee cups. Steam rose from the cup's air hole as it hit the brisk air. Roger hoped they would toss the cups in the nearby trash bin. Maybe they would leave a few sips or more; but they passed by it, talking about something he could not care less about.

Another group of noises followed. Two youth soccer teams took the field in front of him accompanied with the whistles of coaches and referees. They began to practice and soccer balls were soon in the air.

It was another day in the park. Every day is the fourth of July for some people, Roger thought.

Roger Waterman was the exception in this park. No one here saw the horrors that he did. No one did what he had to do to survive like he did. To everyone else here, it was a picnic, a walk in the park like the yuppie couple. What were their worries? The color of the bridesmaid dresses? How many in the wedding party? Stretch limo or bus?

Roger Waterman got out of hell somehow. But he was marked, and the Hunter's were after him. He had to stay hidden, out of sight and off the grid. That would be the only way. He had to move about, maybe venture from city to city, small town to small town.

Secret writings were everywhere. Only Roger could decipher them, only he could see the hidden clues. The Hunter's communicated among themselves with secret hand messages. Roger could spot them almost anywhere. It would be the slightest move of the finger while drinking coffee at a café, readjusting their glasses to look at him or signal another Hunter.

It was their mission to recapture Roger and take him back to hell. So far he was able to outwit them, as long as he stayed hidden, out of sight, off the grid.

Satan's Secret Servicemen had their own agenda, of course. Stir the world into mass chaos. Turn people against each other. They thrived on murder and destruction of any kind. As long as people suffered, they were winning.

"Look at them," he said to himself. "They have no clue. Their lives are being destroyed before their very eyes and they do not see it. Their world is being taken over and all they care about is their coffee."

Roger heard a familiar voice and turned toward it. They found him. Satan's Hunters from Hell found him.

"Roger, it's me," the man said. "It's Doctor Corman from the shelter. I came to see how you were doing. We couldn't find you for a long time."

That's who the man said he was. That's where he says he's from. Roger looked at him through a suspicious glare.

"We brought you some blankets, food, and some water." The man and his accomplice put them down and walked a few steps back. "Why don't you come back to the shelter with us, get a hot shower and your clothes washed?"

"I'm o.k." Roger answered. "I'm o.k."

Roger Waterman waited for them to leave before he took the food and water. He ate quickly; occasionally looking over his shoulder's to see if anyone else recognized him. He kept a careful watch for any of Satan's Hunters, impersonating humans and wanting to take him back.

It was just another day in the park, always like the fourth of July.

The 4th of July Celebration Is History
Bill McKinley
(578 words)

Mr. Don Gibson was a world-renowned sailor who took hundreds of oceanic voyages, many with his long-time girlfriend and harbor barmaid, Brandy.

Ten years ago, while sailing on the South China Sea with his full crew, Captain Don broke the bad news to Brandy by telling her that although she was a fine girl and would be a good wife, his life and love was the sea.

Brandy tore the braided silver locket Don brought home for her from the north of Spain and threw it overboard.

"Why didn't you tell me you were taking me to the Sea of Heartbreak?" she shouted, immediately prior to jumping into the angry waters. Don and his men watched helplessly as the rough current consumed her instantly.

Mr. Gibson lived in seclusion for two years; then, he resurfaced unexpectedly and landed a job as a disc jockey for a large California radio station. He became an overnight national sensation and gave popular DJs Wolfman Jack and Casey Kasem a run for their money.

Entering his fourth year of stardom, one night Don locked the door to his studio and played *Beyond the Sea* by Bobby Darin on the air for four hours non-stop, while singing along to the words referencing her watching for him beyond the sea, and their futuristic meeting beyond the shore, which would result in the culmination of his sailing days.

Naturally, this incident ended Don's radio career and resulted in his admission to a mental hospital. While there, he was permitted to play his CDs, and after only several weeks, he started playing songs referring to death; for example: *Moody River* by Pat Boone, *Honey* by Bobby Goldsboro, and *Tell Laura I Love Her* by Paul Peterson.

****

That's where I entered the picture. My name is Ruby Tuesday, and I became Mr. Gibson's personal psychiatrist. The following is what has been going on in my world for the past five years and what happened in my world only yesterday:

It took me three years to assist Don out of his deep depression. I told him constantly that every day is another day in the park and every day IS the 4th of July. Every day I played *Saturday in the Park*, a big hit by Chicago in 1972, over and over again while Don and I walked in MacArthur Park.

Although not ready to rejoin society, in Don's world, he did believe that every day was July 4th, and he started listening to happy songs again every day during our treks for the last two years, such as: *A Beautiful Morning* by The Rascals, *I Believe in Music* by Gallery, and *Walkin' in the Sunshine* by Roger Miller.

Yesterday morning, while strolling to the hospital in the early morning rain to begin another week of tête-à-têtes with my favorite patient, I looked up and didn't see Don at his window from where he waved to me most days.

When I neared his private room, as on most mornings, I could hear music emanating from his CD player, which put an immediate smile on my face.

When I entered, Mr. Gibson was face down on his bed. He was dead of an apparent suicide.

Don was right—no more sailing.

Regrettably, the daily 4th of July celebrations are history.

Oh yes, by the way, the song that was playing in the background when I found Don yesterday was the depressing, *Rainy Days and Mondays* by The Carpenters.

Prompt # 18

I don't feel as relaxed as I normally do...

This prompt is briefer than most of the others. Likewise the two stories which were selected are extremely short. A story must have a concise beginning, middle, and end. Short fiction of up to approximately 500 – 1000 words is considered "flash fiction." Examples are found throughout most of the book.

Other extreme short story forms are:

6-Word Story – using 6 words

Twitterture – using 140 characters or less

Dribble – using 50 words or less

Drabble – using 100 words or less

When a story has 400 words or less, it is considered "micro fiction." Since neither story for this prompt is over 170 words, they both fall into this category.

Another unusual coincidence between these is that, although the authors did not know each other, they followed a loosely connected theme of entrapment. The way most of the prompts included in this book are presented, it is easy to understand how the writers chose similar paths. However, this prompt is so sparse that it could lead a writer in an incalculable number of ways.

That Funny Feeling
Vicki Grey
(163 words)

"What's the matter with you," Reince asked.

"I don't know - I don't feel as relaxed as I usually do," Gina responded.

"Don't you feel well?"

"Yeah, I guess. I just have this 'feeling' I can't shake."

"Look, sweetie, the sun is shining, the sky is blue, and we're together. What more can you ask for??"

"Okay, okay," she nodded. "It's a great day. I just 'feel' something dreadful is coming..." Gina bit her fingernail.

"You call this dreadful?" Reince scooped her up into his arms.

Gina smiled, putting her arms around his neck.

"Mmm," she murmured into his neck. "Baby, you rock my world."

"No! It's not me," he cried.

Gina looked confused as Reince put her back on her feet.

She felt it then under feet. "Earthquake," she screamed.

The earth began to split open and as she screamed, trying desperately to maintain her balance, she fell backward into the crevasse. Another temblor and the rift closed again, entombing Gina forever.

Silence Was Golden

Bill McKinley
(169 words)

I don't feel as relaxed as I normally do.

Although my boring world has reverted to one of tranquility again, the customary quietness was interrupted earlier by muffled outside sensations. It sounded like voices or echoes, albeit, I wasn't positive, since I hadn't heard any noises—let alone spoken words—for a very long time.

Suddenly, a loud pounding reverberation like an earthquake replaced the oral vibrations. I seemed to be flying in space as the back and forth thudding continued. Occasionally, momentary calmness revisited, only to be disturbed by the abrupt recurrence of the banging and my perception of being airborne.

Then, without warning, stillness returned. The enclosed silence I've grown accustomed to and my feelings of hopelessness, abandonment, and loneliness are also back.

With a dizzying headache, I eye the antiseptic, misty haze that surrounds me.

No, I won't despair. Maybe my visitors will reappear.

If not, I'll continue to be resigned to my fate.

Maybe things could be worse than spending life inside a Ping-Pong ball.

Prompt # 19

*You're shopping for groceries when
the bananas tell you to _____ or _____.
Describe how you handle the situation.*

This prompt's chapter includes the expected strange imaginings from a number of writers. It also contains the only poem that was chosen to be included in the anthology.

In a world where anything can happen, it is not impossible to believe that somewhere, somehow, produce may speak to you. Alright, it is rather impossible to believe that the actual fruit is talking. However, through inner voice, microphones, and perhaps a shift in reality, the authors created plausible possibilities.

The first offering is a poem with only a number for a title. It has more meaning and depth than the stories.

The second story has a curveball as twisted as the concept of talking bananas.

Fans of Rod Sterling's classic television show *The Twilight Zone* will enjoy the third story presented in this section.

1 9
Susanna Fussenegger
(69 words)

Little basket, groceries
Filling only daily needs
Shrinking waistlines empty nest
No deep cart or family fest

Shopping in the produce isle
There bananas piled on tile
"You better grab us" yells a bunch
Or your heart will surely crunch

Not from heart ache, broken soul
Potassium intake is your goal
We bananas know that better
Don't care if we make you fatter

The Twilight Hour
J.J. Hardic

(832 words)

It was getting dark, that time of day where the sun is disappearing, but there was an eerie array of colors that painted the sky. It produced a feeling of uneasiness and anxiety for some reason. You got that feeling of not wanting to walk into a building for fear of something happening. Little did I know that my fear would soon take form.

I went grocery shopping at the same store where I have always gone. It wasn't big compared to today's super stores, but they always had a nice selection of food. I had a craving for ice cream and put it in my cart. For some reason a banana split came to mind. It probably would have been easier just to stop at an ice cream stand, but I thought I could make banana splits for the rest of the week.

The fresh fruits and vegetables were against the wall close to a little sitting area, which served coffee. A fine mist of water sprayed the vegetables. I passed them and stood in front of the bananas. It had to be the perfect bunch, not too ripe or they'll go brown and soggy quickly. And, certainly not too green, they are not ripe yet and would not taste good. I picked up several bunches and put them down. I found a bunch the exact color and feel I was looking for, and then it happened.

The bananas spoke to me.

"Put me down. You don't want to eat me."

I was shocked and turned around but no one was there. I looked up for a hidden microphone thinking it was some type of joke.

"Put me down," they said, "or I'll have you trip on me and

you'll break your leg."

"Is this a joke? Are you talking to me?"

"No. I'm talking to the clown behind you. Of course I'm talking to you, you idiot."

I did not know what to do so I dropped the bunch of bananas. Then I saw it, there were two markings on the outer two bananas, and several lines running across the bottom. They made a smiley face. It was ghastly in a way and I backed up a step.

"This has got to be a joke. There's a hidden camera here somewhere, or some ventriloquist throwing his voice."

"Hey, John," the bananas said. "Are you on drugs? Did you take any LSD or anything?"

"No."

"Well maybe you should consider some anti-psychotics. You're the one carrying on a conversation with a bunch of Cavendish bananas."

Then I heard laughter. It was coming from the apples one bin over. I took two steps over and could only stare at them

"I don't believe this," I said.

"What did he say Jonathan?" the Granny Smith Apple said. "I'm hard of hearing."

"He said he does not believe this," the Jonathan Apple replied.

"Take me," the Paula Red interrupted in a sexy and sultry voice. The apple rolled over the others and stopped directly in front of me.

"I saw him first. Me. Take me," the Pink Lady Apple said in a southern accent. She rolled up next to the Paula Red.

"No. Me. I'm delicious. You can make a pie or put caramel on me," the Golden Delicious Apple jumped in.

"I'm more Delicious," the Red Delicious Apple argued.

"Enough," I said. "I feel like I'm in a Muppet Movie. All the fruits are talking to me."

"This is so touching, I want to cry." The hard voice of the onion added.

I did not know what to do. Were they really talking to me? Was I on some video show? Should I push on to the poultry and fish aisle? Fear and anxiety won. I had to get out as quickly as I could. I left my buggy with the ice cream in it and turned around.

I took two steps and froze.

Sitting there at the coffee stand was a frog puppet with his legs crossed drinking coffee. Across from him sat a man in a black suit with coffee and a cigarette in front of him. The frog looked at me and then at his watch.

"I get a fifteen minute break just like everyone else. It's in the Union contract."

"O.K." was the only thing that I was able to get out. Then the dark haired man spoke.

"It started out just like any other day for John, until he decided to go shopping. He reached for the Cavendish bananas, but Cavendish had other plans than being split and covered with ice cream, nuts and topped off with a cherry. It was a lost sixty minutes for John, caught between real live talking fruits and vegetables. Each with their own special personality.

"It was John's own personal Twilight Hour in which he realized that very thing."

I have never eaten a banana or looked at fruits and vegetables the same, and I have never been back to that store.

The Singing Bananas
Jenifer McNamara
(279 words)

You're shopping for groceries when the bananas tell you to buy me some peanuts and cracker-jack or take me out to the ole ballgame. You look at the bananas and all around the small store in disbelief. They're singing one of your favorite songs. *Someone's being a big tease*, you thought. So, you stand in front of the banana table looking this way and that way for someone. Then you stand on your soapbox and conduct the bananas lovely voices with your magic baton. Still no one attends to you at all.

Are these marvelous bananas really singing? Is this some kind of miracle? Again, you look to your right and to your left. Then a couple, a man and a woman, approaches you.

"Is that singing I hear?" asks the man.

"Yes, the bananas are singing "Take Me Out to the Ole Ballgame," you say.

"Thank heavens! We thought we were the only ones," says the man.

All three of you stand around and listen to the bananas sing. Then you take a photo of the singing bananas on your cell phone and send it to the neighborhood news. A few more people gather and listen to the singing bananas.

"Where's the singing bananas," shouts a woman from the front of the store. A few minutes later, a cameraman and his crew appear. They film the singing bananas and interview everyone. Then the woman shouts, "It's a wrap. Look for yourselves on the five o'clock news," and hands everyone tickets to the next home ballgame.

So, it ends, the singing bananas are going to be on the television show, American Idol, and you are going to a ballgame.

Prompt # 20

I might lose it in the chaos.
What is "it"?
How can I get "it" back?

Nearly everyone can relate to "losing it" when life becomes chaotic and unbalanced. Day-to-day uncertainties take on an overwhelming urgency. This is particularly true when the upheaval relates to parenting and aging, both of which are used in the following pair of stories.

One of the "rules" for the contest part of this book was to write a story, memoir, or poem using the prompts...and under 1,000 words.

The second story in this section overshot the word limit. As mentioned in previous chapters, sometimes it is acceptable to bend the guidelines of a prompt.

The other piece is a tightly written bit of flash fiction coming in under 340 words. They balance the chapter while examining ways to balance life.

Frustration
Kerry E.B. Black
(332 words)

Sitting in Oakland's traffic shot Courtney's schedule to heck. Another pajama-wearing co-ed crossed the street at a leisurely pace, unconcerned by the crush of cars and busses rushing the light. Courtney squeezed her eyes tight and gripped the steering wheel until her knuckles ached. The girl made it across the street uninjured, despite the other motorists.

Her kids bickered in the back of the car. The slow travelling pace generated no air circulation to move the hot July air, and Courtney could see the baby's heat rash creeping around her belly and thighs. Bad time for the a/c to break.

A squealing complaint, and Courtney said, "Stop touching your brother's ear." Her ten-year-old smiled like The Joker in a card deck. The five-year-old whined, "She's doing it again."

"Mom, I have to pee."

"P-U! The baby's diaper stinks."

"You stink!"

"Do not!"

The baby kicked her ruddy legs and fussed as the complaints mounted. Courtney felt buried in unhappy words, drowning in dissatisfaction. She gasped when a PAT bus cut her off, nearly clipping her front quarter panel. Her already tight grip on the steering wheel tightened, and her temper snapped. She screamed out the window, face red as the blazing sun over the foggy city.

The kids, disused to profanity and displays of anger, fell silent, stunned and wide-eyed. Even the baby gasped bag sobs, frozen in fisted wonder.

Courtney's hair billowed like a deranged Muppet's fur as she gestured and yelled. The traffic crept forward. Courtney's nostrils continued to flare, desperate for oxygen. Her joints ached, and tears sprung to her eyes. Fearful eyes stared from the rear view and child safety mirrors.

Trying to remember what she said during her furious outburst, she blushed. What had she done? What kind of example did she set? She whispered a guilt-heavy, "I'm sorry, kids."

The three children relaxed into their seats. The five-year-old giggled. "Mommy called the bus driver a pooh-pooh head."

Losing It
Megan Vance
(1520 words)

Eighty-five year old Luella Jean Wittenmeyer trembled as she stood under the blue light special sign in line at the Bumpertown Big K. It whirled and swirled around her overwhelmed senses, making her withered body suddenly feel dizzy when the loudspeaker blared. All the shoppers must, "hurry, hurry over!" while there was still time to pick up the buy one get two special.

"Buy one, get two what?" Luella wiped sweat beading on her forehead as she rifled through her overstuffed purse. "Just what do they want me to buy?" she said to no one in particular.

No one paid attention anyway. Luella had forgotten to put in her hearing aids this morning so she couldn't make out what the special was. Behind her stood a very pregnant woman with two tow headed twin girls. With dirty faces they screamed from inside of the woman's grocery cart. They clamored for the blue light special, whatever it was.

"Mommeee, I hungy,"screeched one with a binky and a torn Minnie Mouse shirt. The excitement was contagious, for it was hot dog day at the Bumpertown Big K. The last Sunday in June, all of Bumpertown shuffled on out to get themselves hot dogs before Big K ran out of their supply. Who could beat a special like buy one, get two? Pregnant Mama didn't pay much attention to her babies' hollers, though. She was too busy texting on her phone with her current boyfriend, who was trying to decide on a bathing suit over in the men's department. The pics he sent of him modeling them had the young Mama mesmerized.

The speaker put out the final call for the dogs, though

Luella did not know it. All she knew that was that darned blue light had just about triggered a stroke. A chubby ten year old boy belted for the line to scoop up the last of the dried up, lukewarm dogs. As she dug around at the bottom of her purse, Luella felt herself suddenly crumpling to the floor. Knocked breathless, a fragile faded flower trampled, she was the last of anyone's concern when the light finally stopped whirling. The brat didn't even notice that he knocked over a frail, elderly woman. He didn't even her cry out for help.

"Aye, yai, yaeeee!" Luella shouted as her bony hip made contact with the hard floor. Dr. Mosely had warned her to take her calcium supplements for a long time, had said her bones were weak. Luella always "meant to" get her bottle of calcium from the drug store down the end of the street, but it seemed she always forgot when she got there what she had gone in for.

The careless shove caused searing pain. She knew instantly that her hip was fractured. After many close calls, Luella was down for the count this time. "Oh, if only I could get back, get back!" she cried, once again to no one in particular. People just scooted around her, shoving in their mouths the last of the wieners, or texting on their phones, taking selfies, or other things that didn't include noticing or even helping any elderly people in the proximity.

She grimaced, grabbing the nearest counter, trying to pull herself to a sitting position, but couldn't. She continued groaning when at last another older woman (way past retirement age herself but unable to retire) adjusted her glasses to see what or who this was, blocking the way to her jewelry counter. Ruthie Jones sold cubic zirconia engagement rings to city folks, whose industry had left their town years ago and mostly survived on welfare.

"Oh my dearie," Ruthie extended her own wrinkled and trembling hand to Luella. "What happened to you Pumpkin?"

"Someone knocked me down. I guess that whirly-light gizmo took away any thought they might have of, of..." her voice trailed off as she wiped some blood off her elbow. "Oh my, I hit my arm too."

"Honey, I am going to call the medics, so you just stay tight where you are," Ruthie soothed.

"Oh no, please just call Harry," and then added under her breath, "even though he'll be furious." In the meantime, she felt herself breaking into a cold sweat and nauseous because of the pain. Her heart pounded outside of her chest.

"Who is Harry?" Ruthie chirped, rubbing her chin.

"My husband," Luella whispered. "I know he'll be hopping mad but I snuck out in the car while he was napping. I wanted to get some, some, oh darn it, now I can't remember what it was I was here to get!" She sobbed. "My daughter keeps telling me I am losing it but I wanted to prove her wrong!"

Ruthie whipped out an older model cell phone and dialed 911, in spite of Luella's pleas. While the room spun around her, a path was finally cleared so the medics could get in and haul Luella off to Bumpertown General, where everyone joked that they loved to bump people off.

"Ma'am, do you have any identification with you?" said a black haired burly medic, who had only stopped by only an hour ago to buy a couple blue-light dogs on his lunch break. "We need to call your first of kin."

"Just call Harry," Luella said as her eyes just wanted to close, her body trembling. The busy shopping center faded in and out and she remembered being a little girl, holding her Mama's hand at the county fair. What was this, she thought she heard her mother, long dead, now calling her name?

Rita Smith, the be-speckled, redheaded Big K manager walked over to make sure there would be no lawsuit over what had just occurred. If there was a lawsuit, there went her job! And then who would support her single family household? The ten year old instigator was long gone with his hot dogs, off again on his bike and down the road without a thought of the trouble he'd caused.

"Oh that's crazy Lu again," she whispered to the medics. "She comes wandering in here anytime her Harry turns his back.

This time she's really gone and done it."

"Well we certainly need to get her to the hospital, or her family might sue the store."

Meanwhile, out in the parking lot Sue Ann, Luella's daughter, the one Luella had recently begun to fear, parked her beat up Toyota truck. Sue Ann huffed and puffed as she loped toward the entrance. She'd seen the ambulance, and suddenly felt a deep pit in her stomach. Earlier in the day, Sue Ann had stopped at the house to check on her folks. She'd observed Harry's car was gone again, with Harry out on the front porch smoking his Marlboro's, guzzling his Bud Light nonchalantly.

How did she know she would find her mother at the store? She knew, because they always fought about that car, and Luella insisting on "getting out of the house *on my own!*" How many times had she argued that Luella could no longer drive, with a huge family blow up always ensuing?

Sue Ann approached the door and saw her mother being carried out on a stretcher.

"Oh mother, what happened *this* time?" she sighed heavily, seeing birdlike Luella curled up on the big stretcher. Luella's hazel eyes were clouded, yet wild with fear and shame.

"I lost it, really lost it this time at the blue light special," Luella whispered, "and this time I know I'm not coming back. But it's OK, Mama wants me to come to her now."

"Just what did you lose?" Sue Ann flipped her ponytail behind her, thinking to herself, maybe *now* they might listen to what she'd been trying to say for the last couple of years. "And what's this talk about Granny? You know she's been gone for ten years now."

"It, I lost *it*! I know that this was my last time to take Harry's car, to come to Big K, to be free. From now on, you'll clip my wings, so I hope I won't make it through surgery. If I can't be free, I may as well die."

Sue Ann shuddered. Suddenly she realized that after all the years she'd lorded it over her mother, bossing her around and offering her opinion when it wasn't wanted, she had caused a rift that could never heal. She'd supposed she would be so happy when she was finally free from her mother's neediness. Strangely she felt only emptiness instead. Like her little mother giving up on the stretcher, Sue Ann slumped down into the well-worn seat of the cab of her truck, her body heaving with sobs. Without Luella, she was only an abandoned child, left on a doorstep with no more roots, no more home.

While the siren blared in the ambulance, it no longer mattered to Luella whether she'd "lost it." Faculties or none, she was done with inconsiderate people, at last joining the others who'd gone on before. Silently, she thanked the nameless boy for knocking her down. Luella Jean Wittenmeyer was heading home.

Prompt # 21

Nature swaps colors...trees are purple,
grass is turquoise, the sky is white.
What does Sally do to solve this mystery?

Before continuing, be aware that the first of these three stories may be difficult for victims of abuse. However, the author does not overuse graphic imagery or intricate details regarding the abuse and deals with the matter in a satisfying manner. The second story takes the reader on an imaginative trip into the world of the arts, and flashes of the 1960s. The third has the feel of a children's story complete with faeries and tricky pixies.

Two of the stories dip into fantasy and horror, although the horror in one is present in human actions and is mildly used by the faeries in the other. The third feels like a dream. All of the stories make for colorful reading thanks to the imaginings of the writers.

A Tear in the Fabric of Time
J.J. Hardic
(996 words)

Sally ran from the house with the shouts of her drunken stepfather calling after her. The ground was wet from dew and cold but Sally did not feel it. She slipped a few times, but caught her balance and headed into the woods.

Sally took a few deep breaths as she ducked behind a tree. Her stepfather stopped at wood's edge. She knew he wouldn't come in, not in his drunken state anyhow. It was that and some of the stories of fairies and other strange happenings. Sally smiled to herself at what she had done, clobbering him a good one with tea kettle. Right on the top of the head.

It was an impulse thing. She hated him when he came home from the mine drunk, and pushed himself on her mother. But he was getting worse. He was more demanding, and more physical. Her mother had tolerated this behavior for a long time,

But, now that Sally was maturing, he was looking at her with those drunken, leering eyes.

A few times this past month he'd come home from the pub and brushed up against her when she went into the kitchen. Tonight she had enough, so she clobbered him. He'd sleep it off; and, in the morning, he'd think it was part of a hangover.

Sally looked up into the sky. She could see between the trees that the moon was large and bright and lit the forest up in some eerie way. Sally noticed something in the distance. It was shiny lights in a row. She walked carefully on the soft ground toward them. They could be lightning bugs; but they did not move and they were stationary side by side in a vertical line.

Sally approached with caution. It was dark beyond the

lines. She could not see through it. The lights glimmered, and seemed to sparkle at times. Sally touched them. They gave off a warm feeling. Then she put her hand inside and pulled it out.

"Hmmm. Interesting."

Sally widened the lights by pushing them apart. The line opened more like a tear in a fabric. Sally stepped inside.

"Oh my stars in heaven, it's true," was all Sally could say. She walked around in a small circle staring at everything. The trees were purple, the grass turquoise, and the sky white. "This is truly amazing." She walked further in, making sure she did not lose sight of the entrance.

"Who are you and what do you want?" the woman's voice said. It was strong and demanding. Sally turned to see a woman in white with long red hair sitting on a stone alter. Large purple and orange plants where all around her.

"Sally. My name is Sally. There was a hole or something, I was being chased and I came in to hide."

"You were being chased?" The woman seemed to take an interest in Sally now. "Were they gruhls or canoblins? There is a hole you say?" Small tiny fairies flew up from behind the woman, their wings as colorful as a butterfly's. "Step forward young woman and tell me everything."

Sally stepped up to the stone alter and told the woman all about her stepfather. She told the woman how he got drunk and abusive with her mother. How he demanded certain things; and, when his obligation was not met, he took it out on her mother physically. She told the woman how he now looked at her the same way. Tonight in another drunken state he came up behind her and put his arms around her waist. She could smell the alcohol and feel his warm breath on her neck. He pressed his lips against her ear and whispered.

That is when she clobbered him with the tea pot.

'Gruhls and canoblins take many forms young Sally." The woman said. "My name is Queen Taris Yolba. Show me this evil man."

As Sally led her to the hole, Queen Yolba broke off a large purple pod hanging from a nearby plant.

"Ah, yes. Every now and then the fabric of time rips. My fairies will repair it; but first, let's take care of your canoblin."

When they entered the house, Sally's stepfather was asleep in a chair. The television was on and several cans of beer lay on a table beside him. Queen Yolba quietly removed the cans and laid the pod down. It magically opened up revealing jagged teeth like structures. It reminded Sally of a Venus Fly Trap. The Queen placed the beer cans inside the pod and motioned for Sally to go into the kitchen.

"I will give you a choice. Come with me to my kingdom. Leave this place for a better world, or stay with your mother and move forward in life without your stepfather." Sally thought for a moment. "You may want to get your mother and leave for a while. You might not want to watch what happens."

Sally's thought was interrupted by a scream of agony and pain, a scream she had never heard before. It sent a shiver up her spine. She ran into the next room to see that the purple Venus Fly Trap had clamped down on her stepfather's arm and was slowly crawling up to his shoulder. He screamed again to get it off but did not move in his chair.

"The toxins in the plant have paralyzed him," Queen Yolba explained. "It will continue to devour him and use his body for nourishment until he becomes part of the plant."

"I have to watch." Sally said. "I have to watch until the end. I want to be the last thing he sees."

The Queen nodded. "You are a strong young woman. You and your mother will be fine now."

As the fairies repaired the tear in the fabric of time, Sally and her mother watched the canoblin of their life disappear.

The Girl With Rose-Colored Glasses
Bill McKinley
(498 words)

"Hey, girlfriend, what's transpiring with you on this lovely morning?" Sally says, putting on her pale crimson-tinted glasses.

"Not much from this end. What about you?"

"I hope you're not still worried about that stupid Y2K problem. Nothing's going to happen to your computer. Say, have you been outside, yet, Brenda?"

"No, I haven't. Why would I rush out today? It's really dark; I think a storm's brewing."

"Whatcha talking about? I'm looking out my bedroom window. The trees are purple, the grass is turquoise, and the sky is white. It's beautiful out. I'm going to take a walk across the Golden Gate. Wanna join me?"

"Sally Kravo, you're stoned again. What the hell did you take this time? I never heard you sounding so bizarre as this. Did you stop painting again?"

"The hell with you. I'm going by myself then," Sally says, abruptly pushing the red button on her cell phone.

A half-hour later, after donning a red blouse and matching skin-tight shorts, she commences her lengthy walk.

After travelling only a short distance, Sally notices a six-foot tall Bulldog coming toward her, walking a small man on a leash. The man is on all fours and his tongue is hanging out, since it is such a muggy day. Ready to pass, the dog says, "Good morning. It sure looks like rain."

"Rain? The sky is a perfect ivory white. You better get your eyeballs checked, dude," the tall redheaded, leggy girl replies. The dog shakes his head and continues his brisk stroll, tugging the man to go faster.

She stops to light a joint, looks up, and eyes a orange tour bus flying through floating, yellow clouds speckled with dark blue polka dots; while nearby, just outside the cumulous puffs, a giraffe is handing a leopard a traffic citation alongside his aqua Cadillac SUV.

Hearing horns blowing on the bridge, she observes an alligator pilot in his Candy apple red Boeing 747 shaking his paw, as he passes the slower pink 757 driven by a old pink frog in the right lane.

She nears the end of the bridge and detects a lavender-colored elephant engaged in a heated discussion with a light blue hippopotamus. The elephant is shaking his trunk up and down, as the hippo twists his head from side-to-side, as if to say, 'no'.

The happy-go-lucky woman turns around and heads back to her luxurious apartment in the city.

Pausing to light up again, Sally Kravo gazes into the dark maroon Golden Gate strait below. About two hundred feet away, she sees the Beatles standing on the burgundy water singing *Yellow Submarine*, surrounded by a small crowd swaying to and fro.

The young artist finishes her smoke and spots a large red dinosaur at a distance, which has turned and is heading in her direction.

Sally decides to jump down to hear the Fab Four up close, rather than engage in a presumed meaningless conversation with the approaching reptile wearing a tangerine-colored tuxedo.

The Sally Saga
Jenifer McNamara
(807 words)

Nature swaps colors. . . trees are purple, grass is turquoise, the sky is white and it makes nine year-old Sally smile. She thinks of the fairies that take care of Spring. While Sally's looking out the front window, she hears her mother and asks, "Mom, how come the trees are purple?"

"Purple trees?" asks Mom and runs to the front window and stands beside Sally. After Mom sees the purple trees, turquoise grass, and white sky, she turns on the television. The mysterious colors attract Sally, and she looks for a magnifying glass.

Sally locates a small magnifying glass, skips out the front door, and sits on the turquoise grass and exams it. After examining, one patch after another, Sally doesn't find an answer for its turquoise color.

So, Sally walks around the house to the backyard. She sits in the turquoise grass and hears humming.

Following the humming, Sally trips and falls. She sees five fairies sitting near a wee purple fairy door in one purple tree. The fairies see her and shrink Sally to fairy size.

"What have you done?" shrieks Sally and looks down at herself. The fairies laugh. Sally runs and falls through the earth onto a large table filled with a feast and surrounded by a family of rabbits.

"So nice of you to drop in. We don't get many visitors," says the rabbit at the head of the table wearing a gray suit. Sally can't believe her ears and bites her tongue. "Would you care to join us in this thankful hour?" asks the same rabbit.

Sally nods. The rabbit nearest grasps her hand with its paw and shows Sally to an empty chair at the large table. She doesn't believe how hungry she is and fills a plate with a lot of food that smells good enough to eat. At the large table, Sally hears the pixies and fairies are at war. They are the ones changing the colors of the sky, trees, grass, and all other things.

After Sally eats everything on her plate, she yawns, and falls asleep. Hours later, Sally wakes.

She cannot move. White ropes hold her tight. Sally fights her way to the dirt wall. She sits against the dirt wall and looks for something sharp to cut the ropes. Sally finds a fork under the table.

Moments later, Sally's free. She climbs out of the rabbit hole. Sally feels on top of the world takes a deep breath, and looks around her backyard. Then Sally looks at the sky and sees the sun's up high. Also, she sees something big and blue flying toward her. Sally waves her arms at the big blue flying thing. It stops a few inches from her.

"Dunt at your service?" says the big blue flying thing.

Sally laughs and asks, "Who are you?"

"I'm Dunt, a knight of the blue-dragonfly table, at your service," says Dunt and bows. Sally climbs onto Dunt's back. Together they soar through the cloudless blue skies.

Then Sally sheds a tear and says, "Dunt, I have something important to tell you." Dunt slows his speed and lands on the petal of a large flower. Sally says, "A fairy attack made me small. I'd like to be myself, a person, or human again."

"Can you help me?"asks Sally.

Dunt puts his wing to his chin and says, "We'll go to the fairy kingdom." Dunt lifts off and flies to the purple trees of the fairy kingdom.

Flying in the purple trees, Dunt spots a wee purple door and lands on the grass near the purple tree's trunk. Dunt knocks on the fairy door. Soon, a fairy greets Sally and Dunt. Dunt explains Sally's problem to the fairy in fairy language. The fairy tells Sally to follow as Dunt waves good-bye. Sally and the fairy enter the small door at the trunk of the purple tree.

Inside the fairy kingdom, Sally's eyes fill with wonder at the sight of so many fairies, bright colors, and the wee furniture. Then the fairy takes Sally to the SunFlower Fairy.

After the SunFlower Fairy hears of Sally's plight, she takes Sally to her small hut and makes some tea and shortbread. Not just any tea, but her own brew of Purple Flower tea. The SunFlower Fairy gives Sally the Purple Flower tea and tells her to drink it. Sally drinks the tea. Then the SunFlower Fairy puts on her sparkly cloak, puts the shortbread into a sack, and tells Sally to follow.

Together they walk to the entrance to the fairy kingdom. They stop at the first purple door, and the SunFlower Fairy hands Sally the sack with the shortbread. The SunFlower Fairy says, "Eat the shortbread and all will be well," and disappears.

Sally eats the shortbread and all is well for a long, long time.

Prompt # 22

Happy Earth Day...you find yourself
in the middle of a clash of protesters.
What are they fighting for?
Who are they fighting against?

Conflicting ideals are a problem in society. Friends and families are often torn apart. Civil unrest causes anxiety for many. While those who blatantly brandish their opinions on controversial topics may become agitated and aggressive, the greatest unease is suffered by those caught in the middle.

A fine example of ways a writer can view and use a prompt is found in the first story in this section. The writer uses her personal voice by writing in first person and her unspoken thoughts are clearly heard in her use of parentheses. While this style of writing is not generally used for works of fiction, it can be useful for those who wish to write engaging memoirs and life stories.

The second story uses imaginary groups to represent actual causes and shows how sometimes small differences of opinion can escalate into riots and conflicts. This has happened throughout history and will continue to happen for all time. The innocent by-stander is often caught in the crossfire, but although things get sticky for the main character, he is able to make it through to the end.

Happy (Down to) Earth Day
Susanna Fussenegger
(451 words)

I find myself in the middle of a clash of protesters. Truth be told not in the middle, really, rather there I am on one side, located near the sliding glass door where I carry the dinner dishes in and out to the porch, and there on the other end are my husband and sons sitting around the picnic table. You would never guess that they just finished a big meal, which usually results in a lean-back, all-is-well-with-the-world satisfaction. No, instead all three of them literally slide towards the edge of our semi comfortable wrought iron chairs talking over each other in an urgent tone.

"No matter what new laws they attempt to write they will never ever keep guns out of the hands from those who intend to have them!"

"Do something about mental health! That is the answer," they practically shout all over each other.

In the meantime, it is my mental health that is in jeopardy as I calmly opine, "I am glad we do not have a gun on the premises right at this moment for I believe they might just use it." (Naaah)

Yes, I do agree that there are truly disturbed individuals out there, but more often than not, there are the ones with the mindless anger. They have envy, they have fear, and what they do not have is self-control. In their haste, they will not fight the impulse to have the upper hand. They are the ones who pull the trigger of the (harmless) "guns that don't kill."

The three men stare at me for a moment then shake their heads giving each other the all-knowing glance that says how little we Nice Mothers really comprehend. Suddenly Aristophanes'

Lysistrata comes to mind, the famous Greek play where women pledged and held back sexual favors from their men until they decided to put an end to the (Peloponnesian) war.

Gosh, too late for that now, but we mothers (Old Women Chorus) could at least decide to stop serving dessert. What do I do next? I start scooping ice cream and walk through that door with a goblet full for each of my men.

Of course, I know that all this is far from laughing matter, which is an understatement of gargantuan proportions, Second Amendment and all.

But, joking aside I am seriously envisioning a Super Mother or a Mother Superior with guts to step up and lead the rest of us who stand there with the dessert trays and the ubiquitous smiles. This SUPER SHE will suddenly scream at the top of her voice, "Son! Put that gun down! Now! Do you hear me?"

What do you mean? Why?

"Because I said so!"

Earth in the Balance
J.J. Hardic
(710 words)

Thomas Johnson sat down with his iced coffee. All he wanted to do was take a break from the ninety degree Pittsburgh heat and humidity. He had already taken his tie off and unbuttoned his collar. Thomas surveyed the coffee shop and reached for his cup.

A group of people, maybe six or seven sat off to his right along the wall and close to windows. They were in some type of passionate conversation.

Thomas raised his cup, anticipating the cool soothing coffee quenching his thirst when another group of people walked in carrying signs. The group along the wall stopped, turned and stared. All was quiet as both groups locked eyes on each other.

Thomas got an uneasy feeling. He looked to the left, then back to the right as the place turned dead quiet. For some reason Thomas felt like he was in the middle of a shootout at the O.K. Corral.

Then it happened.

"You're killing the Earth," a woman who had just walked in said. She was wearing a fluorescent green shirt.

A large burly man turned around in his chair. He had a big bushy moustache that covered his upper lip. "We're not the ones killing the earth, it's you and your ilk."

The group in the fluorescent green shirts stopped and surrounded the woman. Lines were being drawn.

"Those grasshoppers you're protecting are nothing but locusts. They can take out a farmers whole crop of corn or wheat.

They're destroying the world's food supply and you're protecting them!"

The woman was clearly agitated. Thomas hoped that she had made her point and would move on, but she stood her ground. The man and his colleagues stood. He was a large fellow with big arms and a beer belly, which his shirt barely covered. It was drab yellow and had a print of the head of a grasshopper on it. He put on a baseball cap that also had the head of a Grasshopper as the logo. This was not going well. Thomas put his iced coffee down and tried to think of an exit strategy. All he wanted to do now was get out of the way.

"Anyone with a functioning brain cell knows that Grasshoppers are full of protein. People from all over the world eat grasshoppers. They are great with honey or dipped in chocolate. Mexicans put them in tacos and burritos."

The large man stepped forward, now an arm's length away from Thomas. "It's you vegetarians who are killing the planet. Plants give off oxygen and oxygen is what humans breathe. By over-eating your fair share of plants you are taking oxygen out of the air. You're suffocating the human race."

That's all the woman in the green needed to hear. She lunged over Thomas and into the burly man with the bushy moustache. He easily tossed her aside as well as two others. The green shirts started hitting and whacking the grasshopper people with their signs.

The next thing Thomas knew, chairs were flying. The shop's patrons ran for the doors and jumped over the counter for protection. Thomas ducked protecting his iced coffee.

Although the entire incident lasted less than five minutes, it seemed like it would never end. Thomas heard sirens and soon the whistles of policemen were in the store. They quickly escorted the protestors outside of the shop and separated them to opposite sides.

Thomas picked his head up and looked about. He was a little shaken but stood and took a few breaths. He maneuvered around the obstacle course of fallen chairs and overturned tables to get outside. He stood a safe distance away, and just as he raised his iced coffee, a policeman walked by, stopped and turned directly into him. Thomas's coffee went flying from his hand right onto his shirt; it followed the seam of his pants down to his shoes and splattered like a water balloon.

"Sorry," the Policeman said. "You!" He pointed to the burly man with the moustache. "Over here and show some I. D." He turned again to Thomas. "By the way, did you see what happened?"

"No." Thomas answered. "My back was turned away," then he left.

Prompt # 23

Sure enough, it was the same crow.
The scar across its beak told her this.
It was one thing to have the bird show up
on her front porch railing every morning,
but the "gifts" he laid on the doormat
were another thing entirely.
She lifted the receiver and dialed.
"Father Anderson? I think you need to see this."

This prompt strongly suggests both sacraments and sacrilege. All three authors of the following pieces dabble in a bit of both to varying degrees.

Crows are renowned for being not only messengers from beyond, but for their penchant for pilfering. Their intelligence is well documented and they are known to remember kindnesses. However, they not only remember harm done to them, they share the information with their peers. A group of crows is called a "murder" for valid reasons. Harm a crow and fear retribution. Show them kindness and you may be surprised at what happens.

The authors offer up surprises of their own by using crows to bring about astonishing endings.

Four and Twenty
Kerry E.B. Black
(693 words)

Mary poached pears and rolled out a crust just as her Grandmother was shown by her grandmother. "This recipe is quite old," Gram had explained. Mary followed the remembered instructions with care, humming a remembered nursery song, "Sing a Song of Sixpence."

A knock interrupted. She wiped flour from her apron and opened the door.

It stood at the edge of her porch, black eyes glinting. Its feathers absorbed the sun, making it a pool of black on a sunny day.

"You again? What do you want?" When she opened the screen door, it cawed and flew away, leaving another sparkling offering on the step. She picked the gem encrusted crucifix and added it to her collection of twenty-three other pieces of ecclesiastical art. The crow always arrived at three.

She dialed the parish priest. "Father Anderson, I think there's something you need to see. Please come by tomorrow around two thirty. Oh, I've made a pie. I'll put on tea.

He arrived, pulling at his white collar and grateful for a cold lemonade. Their small talk over poached pear pie felt strained.

"How's the family?" Father Anderson asked. Although they departed quietly, they'd left the church due to philosophical differences. She guessed from the tone of the pervasive question, Father Anderson smarted at their absence.

"They're well. How's the Children's Ministry?"

His eyebrows raised. She'd left youth ministry when she

took a position at the local college, professor of history and literature, with an emphasis on international folklore and fairytales. "They're struggling a bit at the moment. Sure would be grateful if you were to return."

She smiled and checked the mantle clock. "We'll see." She wiped her lips on a napkin. "I have to show you something." She guided him to her study. Atop a side table rested the treasures brought by her bird visitor. The religious items included a hand-painted icon, a miniature crucifix, and a rosary. All the items looked antique and valuable.

His brow furrowed. "Where'd you get these?"

She checked her wristwatch. 2:55. She motioned to a seat. "You'll see in a couple minutes."

He touched a cassock. "This looks like Father Carmine's." A crystal vial of holy water glinted. An incense burner dangled from a chain. A candle smelled of myrrh. "Where'd you say you got these?"

As the grandfather clock in the living room chimed the hour, the anticipated knock came.

The crow hovered over the gift, the twenty-fourth. An ornate key on a red velvet ribbon caused Father Anderson's gasp. "I'm pretty sure that's the key to the robes closet. Why's the bird have it? How'd it get it?"

Mary thanked the bird. "I think I have the message now." It cawed and flew off.

Mary asked Father, "Do you know the reported meaning behind "Sing a Song of Sixpence"?"

Father retrieved the key, face crinkled with wonder. "No."

"Way back, the King sanctioned the church and seized its holdings."

Father Anderson's head snapped up, his eyes sharp and clear. "Like the local government's trying to do. Impose taxes on our properties and foreclose if we can't pay."

"Four and twenty." She tapped her temple with a finger. "Maybe if you band together, unify your voices, the government wouldn't be able to change the law."

Father Anderson's shoulders drooped. "There are times we can barely have a civil conversation let alone agree to work together."

She set a hand on his. He started at the contact. "I think we have to try. Here's an idea. Host a reception. Invite them all. I bet if you put your minds to it, you can work this out." She smiled. "You can use the faculty reception hall at the school, and I'll bake pie."

He licked his lips. "Your pie is a pretty great motivator."

They laughed.

"And you can return these." She pointed to the table and the religious items.

He twisted the key's cord around his fingers. "So, why'd the bird bring these to you?"

Mary shrugged. "Maybe because I listened to it, and I remember the old stories."

The smell of pie made his stomach growl. "I guess we should count that a blessing."

The Messenger
Estie Drum
(567 words)

She mourned him for the required time. She believed her soul was finally healing.

"It started three days ago," she told Father Anderson.

"Tell me about it," he said.

"I saw it when I went out to get the morning paper. It was lying right where he used to put his shoes, a single yellow rose. I looked around but didn't see anyone. I heard a crow. It sounded strange like it was singing. But crows don't sing do they? The tune sounded familiar. I couldn't place it. The crow was sitting on my porch railing. Its beak had a zigzag scar, looked just like the scar on John's nose."

"Then what happened?"

"The next day, I found a fig leaf lying in the same spot. John used to joke that we would wear fig leaves in Heaven. And, you know, yellow roses are my favorite."

"Hmmm...."

"The next day a string of golden bells was lying there. The crow sitting on the railing, I knew it was the same one because of the scar."

"Do the bells have any significance?"

"I used to collect bells when I was a girl. In fact, I think I have something similar to that string."

"Have you gotten anything else?"

"Why yes, a blue ribbon, saw it a few minutes before you came. I wore one in my hair the night John and I met."

"And that's all?"

"Yes, but I have gotten something every day since that first day."

"Let me think on these things. Please call me if anything else turns up or if you need me."

"Yes of course, you'd be the first I'd call, thank you for coming."

Three days later she debated about calling Father Anderson. Finally she lifted the receiver and dialed.

"Father Anderson? I think you need to see this."

"I'll be right there. Are you alright?"

"Yes. Please come."

She opened the door to let him in then showed him the photo.

"I got a pile of shiny pennies the day after you left. Of course the crow was there with his jagged beak. The photo came yesterday."

Father Anderson lifted the photo. It was a younger, smiling Jill, a blue ribbon in her hair, her arms full of yellow roses.

"Have you seen this photo before?" he asked her.

"Yes, but it was torn in half, the dog chewed it shortly after John took it. I thought it was thrown out."

"Did you get anything today?"

"Yes, this," she said as she handed him the paper.

He took it and read:

> *Yellow Roses for my fair lady*
> *Fig leaves to help her believe*
> *Bells of gold her heart to hold*
> *Ribbons blue to make her true*
> *Pennies from heaven to bless her haven*
> *Picture Perfect was my fair lady*

Father Anderson set the paper down. "I think you have been given a very special gift."

"But, Father, that last line: 'W*as my fair lady.*' What is he saying? How has he done this? A crow, why? Why a crow?"

"You know that we will all walk the path John has taken. I think he is telling you to keep believing, hold your heart true until that time comes for you. How he has done this? Well, we know God works in His own sphere not bound by our laws, it is not ours to know but to accept."

Confession
Dana Kerkentzes
(999 words)

Sure enough, it was the same crow. The scar across its beak told her this. It was one thing to have the bird show up on her front porch railing every morning, but the "gifts" he laid on the doormat were another thing entirely.

She lifted the receiver and dialed.

"Father Anderson? I think you need to see this."

Her hands shook as she returned the phone to its cradle and walked back to the living room. She could see the bird was still there, his black eyes peering in as though waiting to be invited inside.

"Go away!" She snatched a pillow from the couch, tossing it at the bird. "Leave me alone!"

The crow only cawed, cocking his slightly to the left. Her phone rang not a second later. She answered, not bothering to check the ID. "When can you be here?"

"I'm just five minutes away," said the priest. "Will you be okay until then?"

She nodded, then dared another glance out the door. It hadn't moved.

"Mary? Are you there?"

"Yes. Thank you." She hung up.

Father Anderson was true to his word, and soon he was kneeling at her door. The trinkets were all laid out in a row. He picked them up one by one, studying each for a moment before returning it gingerly to the ground. "I'm sorry. I don't understand. Are these Jacob's things?"

"Yes. All the stuff I buried with him. His glasses. His G.I.

Joes. The photo of us on the boat. He died two weeks after that picture. I put it in his casket. Buried it in the ground."

Father Anderson stood. He reached into his pocket and put on his own glasses. "What you're telling me here is impossible."

"Impossible. But yet it happened."

"Mary, I don't believe..."

"I know it's doesn't make sense, but..."

The priest held up his hand, quieting her. "Mary." He sighed. "What if we close this door and go sit here on the couch and pray together. What do you say?" He reached out to lay a hand on her shoulder, but resisted the temptation.

"No, no prayers. I called you here so I could confess."

"Confess?"

"Yes. I've sinned. And this time I might not be forgiven."

"Mary, surely you haven't..."

She shook her head. "Let me explain. There was this book in the library. It was old. Leather bound, hand-stitched, that sort of thing. No title that I could make out, but there was a crow on the cover. *That* crow." She pointed out the door.

Father Anderson sighed and guided her to the couch. Her eyes, he noticed now, were tired, her hair unkempt and greasy. She smelled of unwashed clothes, and he wondered when she last showered.

"The book said crows are omens. They foretell death." Her voice was calm. Her eyes betrayed her fear, darting back and forth between the priest and the door. "I saw crows before Jacob's death, everywhere I went. Then, the cops came. Do you know what that's like for a mother? To see police at your doorstep?"

The priest shook his head.

"Like a kick to your chest. No. Like being sucked into hell. But, colder. Much colder." She shuddered then, wrapping her arms about herself. "The crow was there too, when they told me he'd died. Until the next morning, then it was gone as though it'd never been.

"You'll remember, we had the funeral that Friday. It was

raining, but the sun was out. I saw it perched on the railing before I even pulled in the drive. The next morning he brought me a lily, followed by a card." She reached into her pocket. "This card." She handed the creased paper to the priest.

"Is this for a library book?"

"Yes. The one I just mentioned."

"And this number written here, 414? What does it mean?"

Mary reached beneath the couch and pulled out the book. It was grander than she had described, a great leather bound tome probably two inches thick. Etched on the cover was the crow. She opened the book to page 414 and handed it to the priest.

He studied it quietly for a moment, the spoke. "Mary, do you know what these are?"

"Yes. They're called runes."

"It's a very ancient alphabet. Do they mean anything to you?"

"Not at first. But I was staring at the page, and as I looked they began to change."

Suddenly, the crow began to flail about, bashing its head against the door. Mary leapt to her feet. "Please, we don't have time. I need to confess." She ran to the door, locking the deadbolt and flinging her back against the smooth wood.

The priest set the book down, open on the coffee table. He approached the woman as one would a wounded deer. "Mary, what do you mean they changed? How? Into what?"

Her eyes were wild now, face porcelain white. She pointed to the coffee table. "See for yourself."

Father Anderson picked up the book. The runes were gone, replaced with English script: *The Ritual of Resurrection*. Father Anderson let the book fall to the ground and for the first time noticed the freshly healed wound on Mary's palm, as though she had cut it in the shape of a star. "Mary, *what* did you do?"

"I..."

They both gasped as the doorbell rang. Neither dared move. Quickly, Father Anderson stole a glance out the window.

The shadow of a boy now eclipsed the spot where the crow once thrashed, in his hand he appeared to hold a flower. *A lily,* thought the priest. He cleared his throat, afraid to speak, "Jacob, son, is that you?"

Three gentle knocks replied, followed by a singular, sharp caw.

"Bless me, Father..." Mary said, smiling, the laugh that followed a mix of complete joy and utter fear. She reached a shaking hand towards the door, opening it before he could stop her. "...for I have sinned."

Prompt # 24

Stephen King is the Keynote Speaker at The California State Writer's Conference. There he's introduced to _____ his own fictional, and quite disturbed, character.

This chapter is a demonstration of the editing process. The first piece is the rough draft that the author submitted. The second one is the version the author sent after making several corrections, edits, and a few changes.

After reading carefully, the author noticed an accidental change in the spelling of the main character.

The edited version has over a hundred more words than the draft. This is due to the way the writer added a few details and/or changed some wording in order to improve the story. Frequently an edited piece is shorter than the original in order to offer a tighter and more concise writing sample. That is not always the case.

Another example of what kind of things to look for when editing is typographical errors that are words. Using a spell-checking program is vital to all written works. However, in pairing such as work/word, form/from, lets/let's, and other similar words, the program will usually not catch the mistake. It is vital that writers check each word after they finish writing.

An excellent way to catch mistakes is by reading the piece aloud. By seeing and hearing it read, the errors can be heard and seen at the same time. Reading aloud also helps the writer to realize that a certain word or phrase may not be working as well as they thought, giving them a chance to make a substitution.

Kings, Queens and Christine's
(Draft)
J.J. Hardic
(978 words)

"It's been a great three days." Stephen King said to the audience. "I really enjoyed the camaraderie, and thanks especially to Jonathan who put this whole thing together. Just remember, no matter what happens to you in life, you can always use it in a story."

The auditorium stood and clapped. Jonathan Kooter took the podium. "Thank you Stephen for a prolific and inspirational three day event. Now lets get you to the airport."

Stephen and Jonathan waded through the mass of humanity shaking hands and getting patted on the back. They made their way to the parking garage that connected to the University's parking garage.

"I've got one more surprise for you Steve." Their foot steps echoed in the garage as they turned a corner. There parked on the end was a 1958 red and white Plymouth Fury. The door opened and a young woman got out. She had brown shoulder length hair and is wearing a white blouse and black skirt.

"What do you think?" Jonathan asked. "I call her Christine"

"Oh beautiful." King said, stopping in his tracks. He had seen obsessive fans before, but this took him completely off guard, especially after spending the past three days with Jonathan. He gave no clue that he was so obsessed with King's writing.

"Oh. And this is my wife Carrie."

"Another coincidence?" King thought to himself.

"Go on, get in, try it out."

Not wanting to offend his host and ride to the airport. Steven got in the car and placed his hands on the steering wheel. He hoped to placate his hosts and move on from there.

The door abruptly shut. The lock went down and seat belts fastened tightly on King's waist and shoulder. It was more of a restraint as it held him tightly. The passenger door opened and Jonathan got in. Carrie climbed into the back. The car started automatically and idled.

"I guess Christine has other plans."

"Don't worry." Carrie added. "I just changed your flight. You'll be taking the red eye back to Boston."

For the next hour Christine drove, Jonathan talked and Steven listened. Carrie leaned forward placing herself between them, admiring her husband's life story. He told King about all the books he practically memorized and how he patterned his life after Steven. All the way down to refurbishing the 58 Plymouth.

It was still light when they pulled down the long dirt driveway just in the outskirts of town. The garage door opened and Christine eased in. The seatbelts unlocked and the door opened.

"Let's see what Mom made for dinner."

"I'd like to call my wife."

"Oh don't worry, I took care of that." Carrie said. "You know, the telekinesis thing, I already sent her a text from your phone. And I shut it off so we won't be disturbed."

Jonathan opened the door to the wood frame house and a large St Bernard leapt out at him barking. He put his paws on Jonathan's shoulder's. Jonathan wrapped his arms around the huge dog and vigorously pet him.

"Alright. Down Cujo. Good boy!"

Cujo ran over to Carrie and licked her face in a frenzy. He jumped on King, but ran back inside when he heard his name being called.

"Sorry Steve. Wanted that to be a surprise too, but let's go in and see what Mom has cooked up."

A wave of smells filled the kitchen, fresh bread, some type

of roast and potatoes. King was now on edge, how many more names from his books will he come across in this bazaar scene?

"This is my Mother Annie. She helps out babysitting our daughter. How was work today Mom?" Annie was dicing and cutting vegetables, she turned to King with the knife raised in front of her. Although she was wearing an apron, Annie wore an all white uniform. "Mom's a nurse at the hospital; she just got off of work."

King gulped and his heart raced. It was the same Annie from his 'Misery' novel. He slowly sank into a chair at the table now realizing that he may not get out of this alive.

"And this is our little princess, Charlene. We call her Charlie for short. Charlie, show Mr. King what you can do."

The little five year old girl held out her hand. A small fire appeared, like a match. The little girl played with it. She made it long and thin and it almost touched the ceiling where burnt marks where. She then made it go from hand to hand like an old slinky toy.

King did not know what to do or say so he just watched. His heart beat fast and he wondered if he would make it out of this horror story alive.

There had to be something else going on here. What was they're motivation for bringing him here?

"Lets get down to business Steve." Jonathan said as his Mother put the food down on the table. "I'm a horror writer but I get nothing but rejections. I can show you the room I pasted them in. Its covered from wall to ceiling."

"That won't be necessary."

"What about a novel written by Steven King AND Jonathan Kooter? Your name can be first." Carrie brought out a large manuscript and dropped it on the table. "Maybe it's the name. You think maybe I should change my name or maybe put Carrie's name on it? Carrie Kooter?"

"I know." Annie interrupted still holding the knife. "Carrie Queen. Then It can be by King and Queen."

They all simultaneously turned their head and stared at Steven awaiting an answer. He looked at them and grinned nervously. His lips quivered ever so slightly.

"Could you please pass the bread and butter." He said.

Hours later Steven King sat on the plane clutching a manuscript written by Carrie Queen.

Kings, Queens and Christines
(Edited version)
J.J. Hardic
(1,082 words)

"It's been a great three days." Stephen King said to the audience. "I really enjoyed the camaraderie, and thanks especially to Jonathan who put this whole thing together. Just remember, no matter what happens to you in life, you can always use it in a story."

The auditorium stood and clapped. Jonathan Kooter took the podium. "Thank you Stephen, for a prolific and inspirational three day event. Now let's get you to the airport."

Stephen and Jonathan waded through the mass of humanity, shaking hands and getting patted on the back. They made their way to the parking garage that connected to the University's Auditorium.

"I've got one more surprise for you Steve." Their footsteps echoed in the garage as they turned a corner. There parked on the end was a 1958 red and white Plymouth Fury.

"What do you think?" Jonathan asked. "I call her Christine"

"Oh beautiful," King said, stopping in his tracks. He had seen obsessive fans before, but this took him completely off guard, especially after spending the past three days with Jonathan. He gave no clue that he was so obsessed with King's writing. The door opened and a young woman got out. She had brown shoulder length hair and wore a white blouse and black skirt.

"Oh, and this is my wife Carrie."

Another coincidence? King thought to himself. *The car's name, and now his wife, identical to the titles in his novel.*

"Go on, get in. Try it out."

Not wanting to offend his host and jeopardize the ride to the airport, Stephen got in the car. When he placed his hands on the steering wheel, the door abruptly shut. The lock went down and the seat belts fastened tightly across King's waist and shoulder. It was more of a restraint as it held him forcefully. The passenger door opened and Jonathan got in. Carrie climbed into the back. The car started automatically and idled.

"I guess Christine has other plans."

"Don't worry." Carrie added. "I just changed your flight. You'll be taking the red eye back to Boston."

For the next hour Christine drove, Jonathan talked and Stephen listened. Carrie leaned forward placing herself between them, admiring her husband's life story. He told King about all the books he practically memorized and how he patterned his life after Stephen. All the way down to refurbishing the '58 Plymouth.

It was still light when they pulled down the long dirt driveway just in the outskirts of town. A lawnmower ran by itself in the front yard keeping a perfect line with the previous cut. The garage door opened and Christine eased in. The seatbelts unlocked and the door opened.

"Let's see what Mom made for dinner."

"I'd like to call my wife."

"Oh don't worry, I took care of that," Carrie said. "You know. The telekinesis thing, I already sent her a text from your phone. And, I shut it off so we won't be disturbed."

Jonathan opened the door to the wood frame house and a large St. Bernard leapt out at him barking. He put his paws on Jonathan's shoulders. Jonathan wrapped his arms around the huge dog and vigorously petted him.

"All right. Down, Cujo. Good boy!"

Cujo ran over to Carrie and licked her face in a frenzy. He jumped on King, but ran back inside when he heard his name called.

"Sorry, Steve. Wanted that to be a surprise too, but let's go in and see what Mom has cooked up."

A wave of smells filled the kitchen, fresh bread, some type of roast and potatoes. King was now on edge, how many more names from his books would he come across in this bizarre scene?

"This is my Mother, Annie." Annie was dicing and cutting vegetables, she turned to King with the knife raised in front of her. Although she was wearing an apron, Annie wore an all white uniform. Mom's a nurse at the hospital."

"Oh, hi. Dinner is almost ready." Annie turned her head as Jonathan lightly kissed her cheek. "I may get called in to work if they get another baby ready to be delivered."

King gulped and his heart raced. It was the same Annie from his 'Misery' novel. He slowly sank into a chair at the table now realizing that he may not get out of this alive.

"And this is our little princess, Charlene. We call her Charlie for short. Charlie, show Mr. King what you can do."

The little five-year-old girl held out her hand. A small fire appeared, like a match. The little girl played with it. She made it long and thin and it almost touched the ceiling were burnt marks where. She then made it go from hand to hand like an old Slinky toy.

King did not know what to do or say so he just watched. His heart beat fast and he wondered if he would make it out of this horror story alive.

There had to be something else going on here. What was their motivation for bringing him here?

"Let's get down to business, Steve," Jonathan said as his Mother put the food down on the table. "I'm a horror writer but I get nothing but rejections. I can show you the room I pasted them in. It's covered from wall to ceiling."

"That won't be necessary."

"What about a novel written by Stephen King AND Jonathan Kooter? Your name can be first." Carrie brought out a large manuscript and dropped it on the table. "Maybe it's the name. You think maybe I should change my name or maybe put Carrie's name on it? Carrie Kooter?"

"I know," Annie interrupted still holding the knife. "Carrie Queen. Then It can be by King and Queen. After all, she was the Prom Queen."

They all simultaneously turned their head and stared at Stephen awaiting an answer. He looked at them and grinned nervously. His lips quivered ever so slightly.

"Could you please pass the bread and butter?" Stephen said to his hosts.

Hours later Stephen King sat on the plane clutching a manuscript written by Carrie Queen. He watched intently as the man sitting across from him methodically ripped small strips of paper from a hardback book.

"I see you're almost done Mr. Tombs," the flight attendant said. "Here, you may need this." She handed the passenger a paper bag. Mr. Tombs looked inside the bag.

"It's just what I needed," he turned toward Stephen and smiled.

Prompt # 25

"Nymph!" the voice yelled.
"What have you done to me? Come back and untie me!"
Who? What? Where? When? Why?

When fantasy takes over, it is impossible to predict what will happen next. There were different paths suggested with this prompt. The writers of the following stories closed their eyes and jumped in. Each went in a different direction. Each path is as unexpected as its climax.

Fiery Nymph
Jenifer McNamara
(445 words)

"Nymph!" the voice yelled. "What have you done to me? Come back and untie me!"

Pytomia ran from the white man she tied up in strands of brown kelp to find the others in his party. They camped on the nymph's sacred ground, and they have to pay even with their lives.

By nightfall, she found the others. She saw them and heard them.

"Where's Jim?" asked Maria.

"I thought he'd be here."

"I'm sure we'll find him tomorrow," said Renaldo.

Cccraack

"Heard that," said Loretta.

"Don't want to hear that again," said Renaldo and crawled into his tent.

Loretta and Maria looked at one another and Loretta said, "Can't sleep. I'll sit by the fire and keep watch."

"I'll sit with you. I'm spooked," said Maria and sat beside Loretta on a big gray flat rock.

Neither of them sat for very long. A few hours later Maria and Loretta were asleep beside the embers of their small fire.

During the night, Pytomia took Renaldo, Loretta, and Maria to the tied up white man and tied them up, too. Pytomia watched over her prisoners and hummed to herself.

At the first rays of light, the prisoners woke. They squirmed and wiggled. Loretta gasped.

Seven foot brown-skinned Pytomia stood and looked at her prisoners eyes. She saw confusion, fear, and fascination at once.

"Who are you?" asked Renaldo. "And what have we done?"

Pytomia faced him and said, "I'm the Caretaker," and looked at the horizon.

"We didn't know that we were trespassing," said Renaldo. Pytomia stared at Renaldo and screamed like a man possessed. Maria and Loretta tried to untie each other. Pytomia wedged herself between and pushed them away from one another.

Jim whispered to Renaldo, "Glad to see your familiar face." Renaldo sighed and thought more about their situation.

Pytomia stood the prisoners in a line and tied them together with strands of brown kelp and pushed them.

Jim, who led the line, moved his legs and started to walk. Loretta, Maria, and Renaldo followed while Pytomia walked with her prisoners and cracked them with a large whip of brown kelp to let them know Pytomia is not to be crossed.

During their trek to Pytomia's village, they walked on a narrow path along the side of a mountain with a five hundred foot drop into a rushing roaring river.

At the halfway point, Jim jumped for his freedom.

Loretta, Maria, and Renaldo followed Jim as this was the hand of fate dealt.

Pytomia reached for them, but her hands only caught a cold breeze. Her nose sniffed only the smells of a river flowing through the crisp cool early morning sunrise.

The Cool Room
Bill McKinley
(831 words)

I was at the Dew Drop Inn on a wintery evening last year, two nights before Christmas. It was near midnight when the prettiest women normally have either gone or are spoken for. I sat alone at the bar sipping my drink, thinking about the boring drive that lay ahead of me.

Out of the blue, a beautiful, sensuous blonde with hair well past her shoulders sat beside me. Considering the lateness of the evening, my natural inhibited thought was "hooker."

"Hi," she said, smiling. I replied in kind. Following the usual chitchat, she asked me to dance. Although unaccustomed to women initiating the Gene Kelly thing, I accepted, and we swayed to three or four slow songs. She was seductive.

The statuesque woman told me she was Greek and that her name was Nympha. She said she wrote music and had an identical twin sister named Nessia. She also mentioned that her father was a rich dentist.

After advising her girlfriend that I was taking her home, we drove to her fancy apartment she shared with Nessia. She showed me her CD collection and extensive library.

"So, I take it that reading is your hobby," I said, matter-of-factly.

"No, I'm a nymph—just like my name."

"What? I'm sorry, I don't follow."

"My name, Nympha, it means bride and nymph. I've never been a bride, but I am a nymph."

"A . . . you don't m . . . "

"That's right; I'm a nymphomaniac."

"C'mon, you're putting me on."

"I'd love to," she replied, with a wide, white-teethed grin.

"Love to what?" I inquired.

"Put you on."

"So, you are putting me on, right?"

"No, but I will."

"You will what?"

"Put you on top," she said, pulling me into the bedroom.

After a night of uninhibited activity in her king-sized bed, I was exhausted. She excused herself and left the bedroom. I started dressing and the vivacious blonde entered the room and threw me down on the bed and had her way with me over and over like there was no tomorrow. She was headstrong and impetuous. I was so spent that I collapsed like a ton of bricks.

When I awoke, I was in a different room—a blue room. The walls and ceiling were painted an identical bright blue that was so intense it actually hurt my eyes. The only things in the room were a blue lamp with a blue shade, a blue bulb, and two blue mattresses. One was on the floor beneath me, and I was leaning against the other, which was mounted to the wall. My arms were tied over my head to the ceiling. I glanced at myself; my entire body below the neck was coated with some unidentifiable blue substance (it wasn't paint) that was the exact color as everything else. There were no windows.

"Nymph!" I yelled, at the top of my lungs. "What have you done to me? Come back and untie me."

The erotic, unclothed blonde entered almost immediately. "What's up, Studmuffin?" she asked, with a sexy voice.

"Unbind me. Where am I? What's this blue stuff all over me?"

"Don't fret, my love. You are in the Cool Room. You should feel special. There aren't many who graduate to the Cool

Room."

"Look, Nympha, I just want to get out of here."

"Oh, I'm Nessia. Nympha had an errand to run. Wow, you were fantastic last night."

"What! Are you saying that . . .?"

"Oh, yes, darling. You did the Nymph sisters last night. As I said, you were special—an anomaly. Very few have had the pleasure of charting the waters individually *and* collectively with the Greek goddesses, Nympha and Nessia, aka, the Nymph sisters."

"Don't tell me . . ."

"Oh, my shy one. You were Mr. Wonderful. We've decided to name you Eros, the Greek God of love." She loosened the blue leather straps to set my arms free.

I heard a sound, and Nympha entered. She handed me a package wrapped in blue (naturally) paper. I tentatively slipped the box from the wrapping and opened it, while the siblings watched with great anticipation. It was a bronze statue of two Greek goddesses in the arms of a Greek god.

"We just had to get you this. It is something to remember our stupendous night together," Nessia, said.

"We will never forget you. Say, what is your name, anyway?" Nympha wondered aloud.

"Fred—just plain old Fred; but, you may call me Eros, if you wish."

****

I haven't told anyone about my extraordinary December rendezvous exactly one year ago tonight; nor, did I ever return to the apartment—until this evening.

An elderly woman said she bought it from a dentist the week after Christmas last year. She couldn't recall his name and had never seen any beautiful blond women in the vicinity.

A dream? Perhaps. Or, was I that great lover, Eros, for a night with two Greek goddesses?

Prompt # 26

You show up for your writing group and
didn't know that there was a new rule...
and you have to leave and return
dressed as _____ or pay a high penalty...

Rules are tricky, and important. It is easy to skim through an email or scroll quickly down to the "agree" button in a website permission form. It is just as easy to ignore or forget about new regulations in a routine meeting.

The first of the three featured stories demonstrate that research can be interesting and can help bring life to a story.

The second shows how quick thinking and creative improvisation are critical in a writer's life.

The third reinforces the truth that it is often more important to be aware of what is not mentioned in the rules as what is.

When writing to submit, whether to a contest, magazine, or publisher, it is vital to always follow the rules. Missing the tiniest detail can make the difference between selection and rejection, especially when the number of submissions is overwhelming. The easiest way to cull the entries is to eliminate any and all who disregard the rules.

Can Clothing Speak?
Louise Eckman
(728 words)

It was Thursday and I was late to my writer's group at the library. Hustling up the stairs, I entered the library classroom. Allen, our group leader, turned to me and said, "Bella, did you forget?" and he touched his vest. Allen was wearing an authentic silken vest embroidered with small images of flowers and leaves. It was an item from America's Revolutionary Era.

"Darn it," I thought, as I remembered we had made a plan that we would all dress for the group in sync with the period of history we were writing about. To make the new rule stick, we would fine people $10 if they did not show up in period clothing. Rather than pay the $10 penalty, I decided to go home and select clothing that fit the 60s era that I was writing about.

Returning home, I went to the bedroom closet where I had a few "hippie" items I could wear. Denim was popular in those days, so I chose a long denim skirt I had and matched it with an old khaki shirt of my husband's which was stained and ripped. Then I remembered I had a long wig that I wore when I acted in a play about the 60s months ago. The wig went well with the outfit – all were long, droopy and dirty! I put on a pair of old leather sandals and was ready to return to the writer's group.

This time, when I walked in the door there were some smiles and nods. A group member was already talking about her novel about the 30s - the Depression Era – a time during which her parents had struggled to survive. The conversation focused on creating a character based on her father. She was not wearing clothing of that era.

"Lori," Allen said, "you forgot to dress appropriately for the era you are writing about."

Lori glanced down at her clothing as if to remember what she was wearing, and then said, "Oh, I forgot...I'll do it next time."

"But this time you will have to pay the penalty," Allen said and laughed. "That $10 will go towards our New Year's Party coming up soon."

Lori looked a little embarrassed, but reached into her purse, pulled out a ten dollar bill and handed it to Allen. "I didn't think we were serious about the costume thing."

"I'll need a dress from the 30s – women didn't wear pants in those days," said Lori. "During World War I, women began to wear pants. Men were off fighting in the war, and women took over their factory jobs. They needed to wear pants for safety. After the war was over, women didn't want to give up their pants. They felt more free and comfortable in them. But pants for women didn't become popular until the 60s."

"I have a pair of bell bottoms from the 60s," I said. "There was a lot of change in the 60s - styles changed dramatically."

We continued by discussing Bill's novel about the Civil War era. He was wearing an army jacket of the Confederacy – something he had worn several times to the group. The collarless coat had closely placed rows of buttons along the front and glowed navy blue even though it was worn and faded at the cuffs. This week's chapter focused on a 16-year-old boy in the novel and his desire to leave his family's plantation and join the army. He longed for the importance he would gain by wearing the Confederate uniform.

"Your army jacket is in great shape," said Allen. "The color is well preserved."

"Uniforms from the Revolutionary era were navy blue also," said Allen. "They were usually matched with red and white. Historically, almost all uniforms were navy blue because that was the predominant dye of history - indigo."

"And it transitioned right into blue jeans," I said. "Indigo dye comes from a tropical pea plant and it tends not to fade. It really lasts!"

"My jacket is from the 1770's," Allen said, pointing at his jacket, which was hanging on his chair back. "And it's still intensely blue."

As I looked around the room, I realized that all of the members except Lori had dressed in period costumes. The images, conflicts and challenges of each historical era came to life because of the costumes people were wearing.

Time Again
J.J. Hardic
(831 words)

Joshua was running late as usual. He looked at his watch as he parked in front of a large Victorian House.

"I'm cutting it close. They'll be starting soon."

He grabbed his bag, ran up the stairs to the porch and pushed the doorbell. It was Phyllis's turn to use her house. They all took turns, but Phyllis's house had all the trappings of a house of horrors, which they all seemed to relish. The door opened and Phyllis stood before him.

"Sorry, I'm running late, as usual."

But, Phyllis only stared and pointed to the living room. Something seemed odd about her tonight. She was dressed in a long black gown that had a high collar up to her neck. Some type of necklace lay on the dress. Her sandy brown hair was pulled up in a tight bun. Joshua entered the living room and saw the others sitting around the table.

"What's going on?" he asked.

"Did you not get the memo?" answered Phyllis.

Joshua looked around the room. Harry was dressed as a clown. His face painted white with triangles around his eyes. Todd was dressed as Count Dracula. Cathy had on a lab coat with red all over it, like she had just come from surgery. Elliott was wearing a mask that resembled an ant, complete with large antennae.

"Apparently not," Todd said in his Count Dracula imitation.

Phyllis ran her hand across Joshua's back keeping it on his shoulder. She came up close to him, their lips almost touching.

"You are a bad boy," she said in a sultry and seductive

voice. "You had to come dressed as your main character or else."

"Or else?"

"The rules are the rules," piped up Harry the Clown. He laughed and pressed a hidden plastic bulb, which spit water from the flower on his lapel.

"Or else you suffer the fate of a character in your story." Cathy said. She then pulled out a large kitchen knife and placed it on the table.

Joshua's mind raced. He only glanced over the last e-mail the writers group sent out. He focused on where the meeting was to be held, and never read the body of the letter. Joshua looked at the gleaming faces of his fellow writers of the macabre.

Where these people really serious about this? These were friends whom he knew for a year now. They met and discussed Edgar Allen Poe, Stephen King and Clive Barker. They were working on their own novels. Would they get into their characters that much that they would forget who they really were and act this out?

The look on their faces said otherwise.

I have to think of something quickly, Joshua thought. They were all smiling at him. Was this their plot the whole time to bring in a newcomer and act out some ghoulish game?

"But I have," Joshua said.

Joshua broke away from Phyllis's touch and walked around the table. He looked at his fellow writers that seemed disappointed that they would not be able to dissect him, or tie him down to some dastardly machine.

"You see," Joshua said. "Although you know me as Josh Tibble, I am really a time traveler from the future, or maybe the past that has come here to solve that problem that has plagued mankind for centuries. Who was Jack, or maybe in this case, Jackie the Ripper?"

"That's not what your story is about," said Phyllis who spoke out of character.

"Ah, but not so, my colleagues," Josh said. He was grasping

for straws now. He had to somehow connect his story, or make it believable if it would help at all. "Although my character in my story is a police detective trying to solve this particular modern day Werewolf murder, he is really a time traveler going through time solving all the strange murders. In time you will know him, I mean me, as H.G. Wells."

Joshua looked around for a response. The others looked at each other for some type of cue. Finally Cathy spoke.

"Oh darn. I so wanted to cut you up."

"Me too," pouted Count Dracula. "I really was looking forward to fresh blood."

Phyllis plopped down in a chair. "Just as I was ready to throw you down on that couch over there. Well, what does everyone have tonight? Anything? H. G.?"

Joshua breathed a sigh of relief. He sat down and smiled at his colleagues.

"I'm a bit tired, you all go first and besides, I just revealed the next part of my story."

"Right," said Cathy. "There's no fun reading it now." She put the knife back in her lab coat.

The group read and critiqued Phyllis's story, then Harry's and Todd's. It was past nine o'clock when they decided to end the meeting. As Joshua left they patted him on the shoulder and back.

"See everyone in two weeks," Todd said in his Dracula voice.

But Joshua never went back.

New Rule
Bill Kemp
(407 words)

The Mile High Writing Club has a way of making good writers become great. It does it by crossing Russian roulette with a talent contest, like America's Idol. Six authors who want to be published climb on board an airplane. As it taxis down the runway, they receive a writing prompt. Ten minutes later, the plane reaches cruising altitude at 5,300 feet. A bell sounds and everyone is instructed to put down their pens. One after another, the six authors read their stories. Then everyone, including the pilot, votes to choose the best and worst story. Ten thousand dollars and a golden trophy shaped like a propeller is awarded for the best story. The author of the story that was voted the worst, is thrown out of the plane.

Works for me. I'm desperate to be published. One of the biggest publishing houses has promised to print the first novel of any author who survives six flights. Gets the competitive juices flowing. I sign up. As I take my seat, I can tell from the chatter that most of the others have done this before. They have extra pens and crisp blue legal pads. One looks to be meditating, another has a crucifix dangling above his tray table.

The writing prompt is impossibly complex. I draw a blank and stare out at the clouds. *Write something. Anything! You don't have to be the best. Just better than at least one of the other writers.* The ground falls away. In a flash I am writing for my life.

Middle of the second page, the bell chimes and the pilot's cheerful voice announces that we are at altitude. Our stories are read in alphabetical order, and being named Thompson, I am next to last. I seem to be flying with a Chekov, London, O'Henry, and a Poe. My competitors are geniuses. I read my story to dead silence.

Then the unfortunate and final author, a Miss Edith Wharton, shares a nauseating story about a cute cat. No surprise about who is the worst. We frogmarched her to the door.

I debated long and hard about returning to the mile high writing group. Every day the mail brought me more rejection slips. Falling from an airplane beats drowning in a forgotten slush pile. I signed up and as we taxied and received our writing prompt I noticed something that I hadn't seen a word about in the rules. Everyone else is wearing a parachute.

Prompt # 27

He stopped the backhoe.
"What the heck is that?" he asked,
looking into the hole he had dug.
There was something white
shining in the sunlight.
"Oh, Lord," he cried. "Is that a skull?"

Digging to build for the future can often bring up things from the past, things that are usually best left undiscovered.

This was a rather peculiar prompt, and the stories it inspired stretched their writer's imagination.

The reader will have to use their imagination to decipher the unique spelling used throughout the first piece.

The second story is very short, with only 369 words. It has potential to grow into a longer piece, but is written in a way that it feels complete as is.

Shorter pieces are often more difficult for writers. Several people who entered their pieces for consideration for this anthology had trouble writing a story in under 1,000 words.

Whut Is Dat Shinen Objeck
Bill McKinley
(787 words)

Im Mose Laffoon en I wanna writ dis heer story en tell yall bout mye frien Jethro who I aint cene roun thesin heer purts fer a koons age. Whut I meen is I aint cene hyd ner har of ol Jethro fer az lonng az I kin rekolect.

Wel Jethro Coe wuz defnitly not da britist bulbb en da boxx az dems reech foke up yunder usta say. Ackshly he wuz kinda stoopid cuz hisn pappy usta be a yellen hay dimwitt en hisn boy wud kum a runnen. Sum wuz sayen he wuz ignert er jus playn tuched enna haid butt I figger he wuz et leest smurt az me cuz we wuz tide inna spellen be en seckund grad.

Jethro wuz afeared of hisn daddy cuz hisn pappy wuz meener then a stryped snak. He wuz kontinuly kussen n screemen. Pervis dats hisn pas nam. He konstinly yeled I dont chaw mye kabbages twicet meenen he dont repeet hisself. Shooot hisn pa wud whup im fer narry a reeson lotsa timz speshluly wen Jet coodnt heer im kallen. Jet wuz harda heeren frum al dems knox he wuz gitten off da noggen. Uh Jet—dat wuz whut I callt im. Kinda klever doantcha theenk.

So fyve yeers go shur seem lik yisterdy Jet wuz a sitten en a digen en stoppd hisn bakhoe quikly.

Whut da heck is dat Jet ask screamen fer hisn pa en luken inta da hol he dun juz digged. Thar wuz sumthen white shinen en da sunlite. O Lord he cride. Den I recollect Jet sayen nex is dat a skul.

Et shure luket lik 1 ta me butt den im not no sinetist er nothen lik dat. Boy im shure hoepen mye recolleckshuns ar acuret.

Pervis wuz inna hous fixen sum slop fer da hogs. He heered Jet en come a runnen all crookit— drunkk az a polcat en hotteren blu blazers. Jet wuz scairt en jus kep pointen ta dat thar hol.

Taint nothen. Yall drugged me outta da keetchen fer dis I. thunk et wuz sumthen critickull.

He spet a beeg messa chaw tabaccer en et wint a fuloten rite onta Jets ovrals.

Pa whut is dat shinen objeck Jet wundered.

Dat dont meen diddley sqat. Et wuz probly a animull Pervis sez. Sumtimes I wisht ya wernt borned. Ya gotta sturt showen yer Daddy sum respeck fer rearen ya up en dat thar holler aftra yer hore ofa muther kikkd da bukkit frum dat yaller feever. Now git bak ta wurk wyl I sturt myken us summ ommlits en polk salid. En whys youns hangen roun im Mose. Yer holden im bak wit yer jawen. Beet et Laffoon elst ul tos ya agin da barnn en fied ya ta da wilt peegs.

Nex mornen Jet tole me Pervis wuz drunkker then Cootey Brown en gott plum loco wenst Jet menchund da haid he cene inna muck. Jet sez he wuz a dreemin in bed en sees hisn pa heet Trixiebelle—dat wuz Jethros ma—in da noggin wit a hoe en den a ax en den seen im throen er inta a deetch bout wer we dun seen da skul. Den--en dis is fer reel--Jet sez he woked up en figgerd et wernt a dreem. He thunk et reely hapen bak wen he wuz a youngun. Jet alsa thunk he rekolectet havven a ollder bruther wen he wuz liddle butt dont no whut becum of im—figgers he kinda vanushed liken hisn ma dun dun. He sez he wuz gonna brang et up wit hisn pappy dat thar nite. To bad deres no kinfok he coulda hav speeked ta. Thays all ded frum badd moonyshin frum up on dem dere hils.

Dat day wuz da las tim I cene Jet. Pervis sez Jet marrd a girl en taun en thay al mooved ta Kaliforny ta go a wurken onna beeg planntayshun.

Dat prevert Pervis Coe cant full ol Mose cuz I knows Jet warnt fonda girls en he shur diddnt lik ta wurk neether. Da way I figgers et Jethro mus bee en da kooler fer kashen alla doze well fary cheks al dem yeers dat wuz sen ta hisn naybur Lum dat up en dide wen hisn donkee kickd im en da haid. I even hellpd Jet plannt Lum rite en hisn oan bak yeard wif al hisn deed muuls en cows.

Umma tayken a jugga hooch daun ta speek wif Pervis tanite. I figger if I kin git im likkered up hill sturt a talken en tel da trooth bout whut hapent ta Jet. I jus hop he wont be kantankruss.

Local newspaper headline two weeks later: ANOTHER TOWN CHARACTER DISAPPEARS.

Skull Visions
Jenifer McNamara
(369 words)

He stopped the backhoe. "What the heck is that?" he asked, looking into the hole he had dug. There was something white and shining in the sunlight. "Oh, Lord." he cried. "Is this a skull?"

He climbed into the hole, picked up the white object and turned it around in his hands. Sure enough, it was a skull. A human skull made of quartz.

Upon climbing out of the hole, the skull gave him visions of glimpses and pictures of things known and unknown to him. The skull vibrated in his hands, and he threw it back into the hole. A loud high-pitched whistle came from the skull. Other workers gathered around the hole.

"Is that a human skull?" asked Thomas as he peered over the hole's edge.

"Yes, and I think it is haunted," said Leon. "Cause when I picked it up I saw things."

"What things?" asked Thomas and glared at him.

"Visions, Pictures of things," said Leon. "I don't understand that sort of stuff so I threw the skull back into the hole.

"Do you remember anything you saw?" asked Thomas.

"Yes, an important person is going to be assassinated, but I don't know who." said Leon and glared back at Thomas. The whistle blew to announce the end of the day. The other workers left Leon and Thomas standing there. "I think we should bury the skull," said Leon.

"I think a museum would be a good place for the skull," said Thomas and went to climb down to where the skull lay. Leon grabbed Thomas by the seat of his pants, pulled him away, and climbed into the hole himself. Leon picked up the skull with his red bandanna covering his right hand. The skull stopped whistling. It didn't give Leon any visions and sat quietly in his palm.

"I'll take care of this," said Leon.

"Have it your way," said Thomas and left Leon standing there. Leon didn't show up for work the next day or the day after.

A few weeks later, Thomas received an envelope with a newspaper clipping about how an attempted assassination of an important businessman was stopped with a note attached that read: *Good Luck and Prosper, Leon.*

Prompt # 28

It's your 30th birthday.
You didn't expect a surprise party,
and you really didn't expect
that _____ would show up.
Who is it? What happens next?

Thirty is a defining age. Some see it as the final division between the fun years of youth and the responsible years of adulthood. Others see it as just another year.

In the 1960s and 1970s rebellious teens followed the mantra "Don't trust anyone over 30." Now all of them are well over thirty. Do they trust themselves?

The three stories in this section are glimpses into the present, future and past. The first is a slice of life by an author who deviates from her frequent meanderings in the realms of fantasy and horror.

The second has a touch of fantasy with a side of life lessons.

The third uses flashback and treats the reader to a different kind of slice of life.

Surprises
Kerry E.B. Black
(217 words)

I hosted a Fourth of July picnic every year, an outdoors gala complete with fireworks and barbeque. Since my birthday isn't until well past mid-month, I never expected to be hosting my own surprise party.

The "surprise" moment happened the year I turned thirty. The sun shone, which was a great relief since I received an unusually large number of "attending" responses to my picnic invitations. The crowd broke into interests. Horseshoes. Volleyball. Bocce. Music. Everyone seemed to be having a great time.

An unfamiliar voice silenced the group. "Where's Kerry? Is Kerry here?" I excused myself and made my way to the source of the raspy inquiries.

Before me hulked a man in a gorilla suit. Huggable Harry. He wrapped me in his malodorous black fur arms and paraded me around my own party, introducing me as "the new thirty-year-old."

For a shy-by-nature person, this proved uncomfortable for me. I smiled, though, trying to be gracious for my guests. At the end, Harry wrapped me in another stinky hug and whispered, "Your sister Heather hired me. Happy birthday."

After he left, I pointed to Heather. She blinked with false innocence.

I hugged her and began to scheme. Since Heather is six years my junior, I had plenty of time to plan for her thirtieth birthday surprise.

Life Lessons
Susanna Fussenegger
(472 words)

It is my 30th. Birthday. I sure did not expect a surprise party, but what I really did not expect was...that my 71 year old self would show up at the door.

There she stood erect, hair blond – no, not shoulder length any more – still fair, and gosh, the look in her eyes! That was the most startling of it all. It was the spitting image of Mom from the Old Country. I sense right away what is coming on this special day of mine. This Senior Me will lift her finger straight into my face and say the mom words: "Don't they have a savings bank in that new country of yours? Your dad and I always put away something for a rainy day and you people over there act as if every day is Christmas day!"

I am turning 30 today for heaven's sake. This should be special , so what exactly am I to do with this Oldster Me predicting coming regrets? Does she not understand that I can - and oh yes I will - afford the bigger house just like my neighbors the Joneses built right next to the best school and the swimming pool. People in the Old Country cannot even imagine that in a matter of few years with diploma in hand I can be a n y t h i n g. Yes ! I can and will join the country club where the grass is definitely greener than you know.

I gingerly open the door wider and I let in the 71 years Old Me and watch her proudly as she walks around taking in the splendor of my home. Is she amazed or is she amused? Hard to tell. There is a certain weariness in her glance. She seems to care, so why is she here to ruin the birthday mood? I resent this and I wish she had not come. I love my life as is and time of course is on my side. Does she know that I am going to get married again and who knows may be have another baby? A girl! She will join my beautiful sons. She will be a princess, she will have everything and more, more, more!

And then my 71 years old self slowly turns around and as if she was reading my mind she reaches into her large bag. She hands me a present, a picture of a young woman in her 20s.

"Oh my! Is this the daughter I am thinking about?"

"Yes" she finally talks. "And she will be so much more sensible than you ever were my dear! She has to be ! She watched you losing much of what you accumulated and was learning right along with you those so called lessons of life."

It's Johnny
Bill McKinley
(823 words)

Bill Frantz heads to the backroom of his favorite Chicago pub on the pretense that it for a surprise birthday party in a half-hour for his friend, Jim Lucas.

"*SURPRISE*," shout about twenty of his softball and work buddies, led by Lucas.

"I thought this was *your* surprise party for hitting the big three-o, Lukey—not mine."

"I knew it would work, since our birthdays are only four days apart," Jim answers.

About an hour later, following the congratulatory handshakes and toasts, Bill notices a stranger sitting alone at the end of the bar. Although he doesn't recognize the man, he thinks he has a somewhat familiar face from a long time ago. He elbows his pal.

"Hey, Lukey, who's that dude on the last stool down there?"

"Beats the hell out of me. This room was supposedly only for us jocks," Lucas says. "Do you want me to tell him to get out?"

"Nah, let the guy alone; he's not bothering anybody. I don't want to ruin my shindig."

"Well, if he helps himself to the food spread later, I'll ask him to skedaddle."

Bill feels uneasy, because every time he glances down the bar, the outsider seems to be staring a hole right through him.

Sipping his drink, Bill is racking his brain trying to place the vaguely familiar sourpuss with penetrating eyes.

All of a sudden, a chill runs through Bill's body, as it comes to him: *It's Johnny!*

TWENTY-TWO YEARS EARLIER

"Mummy, I have to poop," Billy Frantz mutters.

"Are you sure? You have a bad cough, and it's cold and storming outside," his mother says.

"I'm sure. But, I hope that scary man with the little eyes who's always watchin' me ain't there. I'm ascared of him; he looks like that killer we just saw in the movie."

"Billy, the gentleman who lives in the addition near the toilet does resemble the man in the picture, but as I've told you before, he won't hurt you. Johnny Stiles can't help his looks. Don't worry; he won't be outside in this weather, honey."

Holding a small penlight in his hand, Billy ascends two flights of unsteady stairs. His guide wavers in the wind, its miniscule beam boomeranging back into his blinking eyes, as he tries to shield them from the rain.

He slowly opens the squeaky wooden door of the decrepit outhouse, and enters the pitch-black structure at the base of a desolate hill.

Cold water sprays his little butt, as he sits on the cracked seat that pinches his skinny cheeks. Freezing in the semi-darkness, he is petrified, still thinking about the ax murderer in the just-concluded film on television.

Suddenly, the door rattles violently, and he becomes motionless, until he realizes it's the howling winter winds.

Just as he starts calming down, Billy hears a scream emanating from the annex where the Peter Lorre double lives. Jumping up, he grasps his pants, opens the screeching door, and tiptoes to the small apartment. Standing on his toes, Billy peeks through the rain-slicked window.

"Please, Johnny, don't beat me no more," Anna cries. "Let me stay. It's you I want—not him."

With a knife in his right hand, Johnny grabs a clothesline from the floor with his left.

He stabs his estranged wife in the chest, and as she falls, strangles her until her limp body slides to the bloody linoleum.

Billy's eyes resemble golf balls, and he coughs several times.

Johnny looks up, grabs the bloody butcher tool, and rushes outside.

Billy darts into the outhouse and latches the feeble eyehook.

Just as a crack of lightning strikes, followed by a cacophonous rumble of thunder, Billy peeps through the small opening and sees the approaching shiny metal weapon held shoulder-high by Pittsburgh's newest murderer. He shivers, but tries to remain quiet, as the footsteps inch closer.

Johnny yanks on the door. The flimsy lock holds.

Johnny peers through the slit.

"Come on out, Billy. I won't hurt you. Why are you always afraid of me?"

Silence.

He pulls violently on the door.

"I'll get you, Billy. You're next, you scaredy-cat, little twerp."

"Who's out there?" the landlady shouts from a window.

Poking his finger through the crack, Johnny whispers, "I'll get you. It may not be tomorrow, next week, or even next year, but I will find you, Billy." Then, he scampers into the woods.

"It's Johnny," the child screams, as he escapes from his temporary prison.

· · ·

Bill Frantz's friends are kibitzing at tables nearby, and he doesn't want to interrupt. Feeling disconcerted and nauseous, he hurries to the restroom.

The birthday boy leans over the sink and throws cold water on his face to regain composure and organize his thoughts.

He hears the door opens softly, followed by a loud clicking of the lock.

"Hello, Billy. Happy final birthday."

Terrified, Bill turns abruptly, and the dazzling blade reflects directly into his eyes.

It's Johnny!

Prompt # 29

"I love my kitty. I love my kitty,"
sang Elspeth, dancing by the creek.
"You're so lame," yelled her brother.
He ran to Elspeth, grabbing her kitten
from her arms and throwing it into the creek.
"Kitty!" she screamed.

A writer's imagination rivals the strongest magic known. Two of the writers selected for this prompt dipped into the realm of fantasy, while the other dove into the deep, dark corners of the human mind.

Sibling rivalry and the special place animals hold in our hearts are at the core of human existence. These stories highlight goodness and evil, revenge and redemption. They seek to reveal the truth.

Rescued
Lorelei Hayden
(855 words)

Adam Dover almost missed it. He scowled as he walked home from the bus stop, his mind seething with aggravation. He was late getting home for the third day that week. Not that he had anything worth coming home to. A silent, stale apartment and a tv dinner. But still.

The sound of hushed sobbing slowed his steps.

"Kitty. Kitty, please come back." The small voice came from beneath a bush. He bent slightly and caught sight of a worn purple sneaker. Dora the Explorer stared at him unnervingly from the side.

It wasn't his problem. He straightened up again.

"Kitty." The voice was almost lost in hiccuping sobs. For a moment, he could see *her* again, screaming and felt a tendril of panic tighten around his chest. He pushed it away and forced her face out of his mind. He had become good at that over the past forty years.

The foot vanished as the owner wiggled around and he cleared his throat. The sobbing stopped and the branches of the bush waved wildly for a moment. A tiny pinched face appeared, streaked with tears and stray tendrils of hair. She couldn't have been more than seven. Just like Elspeth--he pushed the thought away.

"Please," she begged. "My kitty needs help."

Adam felt an unexpected softness tug at his heart. "Here," he said gruffly, pulling aside a branch and offering her his hand, "let me see." She obediently crawled out and let him take her place.

He tore his sleeve on a branch and finally managed to push his way through the bushes to the other side, stopping just before he tumbled into creek. A rangy cat, as dirty and thin as its owner, stared up at him. It crouched in the soft mud by the water's edge, it's eyes shadowed with fear.

The rushing water brought flashes of memory tumbling back into his head, too quickly to stop them.

. . .

His sister, Elspeth, dancing by the river. The yellow ribbons on her dress floated in in the air as she twirled, holding the little grey kitten up and singing to it.

The feeling of power as he snatched the kitten from her and held it over the water. His cutting words. Her sobs.

And then--it had been forty years since he had been able to face the 'and then.' The world slowed down. The sudden pain as the kitten raked its claws across his face, bringing a thin line of crimson beads to the surface. Her screams as he let go. And then--

The panic, tightening around his chest as he stood frozen, watching Elspeth step off the embankment, get swept away by the current.

He hadn't even tried to go after her. He couldn't force his twelve-year-old body to do anything but watch as the yellow dress swirled away.

They found her body three days later.

. . .

He stood, shaking in the mud until a small voice cut into his thoughts. "Can you save him, mister?"

The little girl appeared beside him, holding her arms across her chest and shivering.

"Stand back," he said, taking off his suit coat and hanging it around her thin shoulders. She pushed her hair back from her forehead as he carefully stepped down the embankment.

The cat's collar had become entangled in a branch. Its body tensed, but it crouched without moving as he carefully untangled the collar and picked it up. Adam could feel the cat's heart beating, like a butterfly's wings, against the palm of his hand.

He climbed back up the embankment and followed the girl out of the bushes. As he handed the kitten to her, his jacket slipped off her shoulders and he noticed bruises across her upper arms. And two small, perfectly round dark scars on one arm.

"Thank you," she whispered, as she took the cat and buried her face blissfully in its dirty fur. He stood debating with himself for a moment. He lived by the rule 'never get involved.' Getting involved in other people's lives hurt.

He had seen scars like that once.

A woman he had once worked with, Catherine, had scars like that, on her arms. She had tried to hide them with long sleeves for years, before she had gained the courage to tell her story. Eventually she had left to become a social worker, with Child Protective Services.

"How did you get hurt?" The words were out of his mouth before he could stop them. His tone was matter-of-fact, as though talking to another adult. He had never learned to talk to children. Hadn't been around them much.

She looked down, rubbing her nose on the cat's head.

He waited.

"My uncle," she said softly. He had to strain to catch the words.

"Have you told your parents?" he asked.

She shook her head, still looking down. "They don't want me. I live with my uncle."

Don't get involved. Go home to your tv dinner.

But then, Elspeth's big blue eyes flashed across his mind. He dug around in his wallet for Catherine's number and dialed.

The King's Choice
J.J. Hardic
(966 words)

"I love my kitty. I love my kitty," sang Elspeth dancing in the creek.

"You're so lame," yelled her brother.

He ran to Elspeth, grabbing her kitten from her arms and throwing it into the creek.

"Kitty!" She screamed and ran after the kitten, slogging and splashing in the water. Then she disappeared where the kitten was thrown.

Thadley panicked and screamed out her name. He got out of the creek and ran to where she disappeared. There he saw the water swirling in a counter clockwise motion.

"It's a sink hole," Thadley said. "She fell into a sink hole." The panic turned into alarm as he called her name, hoping that she would resurface. He could then account for her drowning; he tried to save her but could not. The stupid kitten fell into the water and she went after it. The alarm now turned into dread. How was he going to explain this?

Thadley waited a long time at the creek side formulating a plan to tell his father, the King. He went to the castle and acted like nothing had happened.

At dinner his father asked where Elspeth was. Thadley coldly responded that she had decided to show her kitten the creek and he decided to play in the woods for a while. When she did not answer his calls, he just assumed that she came back to the castle. The King sat back in his chair and grew concerned. His wife touched his arm out of worry.

The King ordered a search party immediately and left the

261

dinner table. Thadley played his part well and followed.

The party searched for hours into the night with torches. They called her name, retracing their steps, looking in the brush for any type of sign, a torn piece of garment, a slight meow of a cat, but nothing, only their own voices and the mist which hung in the air with each breath they took.

Thadley stood close by his father the entire time knowing the outcome. At daybreak, the King went back to the castle and ordered a fresh squad of guards to continue searching.

After days of the same news, the King fell into a deep depression. He feared the worst. His precious daughter Elspeth was gone.

Elspeth's disappearance took its toll on the King's health over the next seventeen years. His wife, the Queen, had died from a flu outbreak ten years earlier, and his strength was failing. Thadley was next in line to rule, and he was getting impatient to become King.

There were rumors that Thadley was cruel to the guards when he did not receive the information he wanted to hear. He was cruel to the horses in the stables when they did not immediately obey him. And, he found it amusing to take whatever he wanted from the villagers.

One day the King looked over his vast Kingdom, and addressed the seas to the north. "I would give anything, anything to have my beloved Elspeth back."

The next day a storm beat the castle walls, the winds howled through the empty spaces in the castle halls. It was dark even though it was mid day. The King and Thadley were having lunch when the wind threw open the large wooden doors. A tall man in a black hooded robe entered the room.

"Who are you? You were not announced! How did you get in here? Come guards!"

"I have news of your daughter," the man said. His voice echoed throughout the cavernous room.

The King held up his arm. "How do you know of my

daughter?"

"Your daughter is safe. She has been with me these past seventeen years. My name does not matter, although I am known by many. The Architect of Time, Wizard, and some people call me Death."

"You're mad," the King responded.

"You said that you would give anything to have your daughter back. I am going to give you that choice." The man in the robe slowly brought his hand out and pointed to the wall. A life size form appeared. It was Elspeth at the age she would be now. She wore a long white dress, adorned with jewels and rubies.

Everyone's eyes were upon her.

"How can this be? What do you want wizard?"

"A life for a life," the robed man said. "Your son is cruel, ruthless and despised by your people. And he is responsible for Elspeth's death."

"He lies!" Thadley sprang to his feet.

The robed man pointed to the wall and they watched the events of the day that Elspeth disappeared unfold.

"Trickery and wizardly magic," Thadley yelled at the Court. "I will not sit here and listen to any more of this."

"I want your son's life in exchange for your daughter's. She has the wisdom, the strength and kindness to rule."

"A woman?" asked The King. "A woman rule a Kingdom? Surely you joke, wizard. Why, I would rather have a toad rule my Kingdom."

"I will return tomorrow for your answer." The wind and rain blew in the great dining room with such force that they had to shield their eyes. Plates and food flew off the long wood table. When the winds died down, the man was gone.

The next day at noon, the robed man stood before the King. Beside him stood a young and grown Elspeth and sitting next to her a full-grown lion. The King had become impatient waiting for Thadley and ordered the guards to bring him.

The doors opened and several guards carried a large

wooden palate. On the palate was a four-foot high toad wearing Thadley's sleep wear.

"You're answer?" asked the robed man.

Familiar
R.F. Gamgee
(382 words)

"I love my kitty. I love my kitty," sang Elspeth, dancing by the creek.

"You're so lame," yelled her brother.

He ran to Elspeth, grabbing her kitten from her arms and throwing it into the creek.

"Kitty!" she screamed, running into the creek after the tiny animal. Luckily, the creek was shallow and the kitten had only submerged for a few seconds. It was shaking, but still breathing, when Elspeth pulled it out and cradled it gently in her arms.

Her brother was laughing. This made Elspeth frown. She looked down at the tiny creature, who was still shaking, and her eyes began stinging with tears.

"How dare you!" she screamed at her brother. The stinging in her eyes overflowed into hot, salty tracks down her cheeks.

"What?" he shrugged, grinning. "It's just a cat."

"*My* kitty!"

Yeah, and it's fine, so stop whining."

Anger bubbled inside of her. It felt as if the water in the creek around her was beginning to churn along with her turbulent emotions. Elspeth's breathing shortened, coming in painful gasps. The tears that had been blurring her vision were suddenly so hot that they hurt.

"Whoa, Elspeth, calm down," her brother raised his hands and began to back away.

"*Leave my kitty alone,*" she growled, her voice sounding deep and raspy, as if her throat had been replaced with sandpaper. "*You will never touch her again.*"

"Okay! Okay, I promise!" her brother was the one crying now.

The water from the creek rose around Elspeth and her kitty. It formed a column around her legs and torso, so hot it was steaming. She stepped through it as if it wasn't there.

"You will never hurt anyone again."

"Yes, yes, never again, promise, yes, yes..." Her brother was babbling.

Elspeth laughed. The sound of her own scratchy laughter hurt her ears. She pointed at the cowering boy and the column of water widened and splashed him. The steaming droplets that landed on him left small red burn marks.

"Please," her brother whimpered. "Elspeth, please..."

"Apologize," she ordered.

"I'm sorry!" he replied instantly.

Elspeth smiled sweetly. The water receded. Her kitty purred in her arms, completely dry, nuzzling close to her chest.

"It's okay!" she assured her brother, and skipped away to play with her kitty somewhere else.

Prompt # 30

Father Carmine is excited about his first position
as assistant pastor at Holy Angels Parish
until he learns that his former lover
is a member of the congregation.

The following three stories take a somewhat similar path, as guided by the prompt, to very diverse endings. While reading them, keep in mind that all names and situations are fictional.

In "What a Surprise," Bill McKinley once again uses creative spelling to convey accent in dialogue. This technique is useful to build the reader's understanding of character and increase interest in the story.

All three have unique twists, which would be spoiled if discussed further in this introduction.

Explore the final chapter and enjoy.

A Strange Sense of Humor
Vicki Grey
(602 words)

He felt blessed, truly blessed. After the rough home, the drugs, heartbreak, the Lord had spoken to him one night. Just a whisper...but enough for him to hear. The next day, he presented himself to Father John at Holy Angels, confessed his many sins, and asked him if it was possible for him, of all people, to become a priest. Father John said yes.

After Father John's recommendation, he managed to get his GED (no screwing around this time) and then seminary. He had served in some tough areas but that was nothing new for him. Now he found himself assigned as an assistant pastor and once again at Holy Angels. How different it felt this time to view the congregation from the altar - to be Father Carmine. His heart was bursting with joy.

The congregation held a reception for him, after mass concluded, in the church hall. Little blue-haired ladies came up to hug him or shake their finger in his face if they knew him. God could truly do miracles to change this one to a priest, they said.

He made the first cut of the cake before one of the ladies took over the duties so he could mingle with the people.

"Father?" said a soft voice, the hand touching his arm.

"Yes, yes, good to meet you," Father Carmine said, turning around.

Carmine froze as he looked at the man. It was him - Jerry! His face turned red.

"Father Carmine, are you alright?" asked a middle-aged woman. "I wanted to introduce you to my grandchildren.

"Yes, uh, grandchildren..." he stuttered, turning away from Jerry.

Carmine had no idea how he made it through the rest of the reception. Jerry! He had left the neighborhood years ago. Why now? Why show up now? What if Jerry talked to Father John? He'd be finished before he started.

He hadn't meant it to happen but Jerry had been his rock during most of those horrible days when he lived at home. Jerry had been the only one to show him any kind of love. When he abruptly left, Carmine had thought about killing himself.

And now, here he was, a priest, and there was Jerry, his lover.

He had to get to Jerry and beg him to keep quiet. All the hard work he had put into becoming a priest, would it be thrown away by his past?

Carmine left the rectory and began walking the old streets of his youth. On a hunch, he headed behind the now defunct warehouse where they used to meet.

Rounding the corner of the building, he saw Jerry ducking through a hole in the wall.

"Oh, Jerry," he thought. "Why now?"

Carmine saw a piece of rebar on the ground and picked it up, holding it behind his leg.

"Jerry," he called softly.

"Carmine! I mean Father!" Jerry smiled and came over to hug him. "I knew you'd come here. I've got a surprise for you."

"And I have one for you, too," Carmine slammed the rebar down on Jerry's head.

Again and again and again until he couldn't raise his arm anymore.

A small album fluttered from Jerry's hand. Carmine picked it up. Inside were wedding pictures and photos of twins. Jerry had married and had a family? This was the surprise?

A darkness came over Carmine as looked at Jerry. So, Jerry had moved on, too. He had killed his only love for nothing.

Carmine looked up at the rafters of the warehouse and the ropes lying everywhere on the ground.

God had a strange sense of humor, he thought.

The New Priest
J.J. Hardic
(927 words)

Father Carmine stood at the pulpit overlooking the congregation. It was his first sermon at Holy Angels Parish. Father Mark was in the hospital recovering from an acute gall bladder attack.

He liked Holy Angels Parish. It was away from the big city and all the big city problems. The parishioners welcomed him with a dinner the first Sunday he was there. He only gave a brief introduction and he and Father Mark shared the sermon.

He was already on a first name basis with the women's auxiliary and the people serving on different committees. He even volunteered his time to be part of the church's drama club for the upcoming spring dessert and drama play.

Father Carmine had just delivered the Bible reading and was talking about the passage when he was distracted by someone dropping a hymnal on the floor. Father Carmine looked at the young man and froze.

It was Robert, his friend from college whom he had a relationship with before deciding on the priesthood.

"What did Jesus mean by this? Well he......."

Father Carmine lost his train of thought. He looked up at the congregation then his notes. What was he talking about? He couldn't remember. Robert had followed him to this small town. What if the people found out?

"Well. What did Jesus mean by this?" His thoughts raced. Where was he in the sermon? Would the congregation suspect something? Somehow he had to recover.

"Well. That could be up for interpretation. Everyone would

get their own special meaning from this."

This was going badly. They were probably thinking "what the heck is talking about?" Father Carmine knew that he had to do something to recompose him, but what?

Father Carmine looked out over the audience trying to avoid looking at Robert. It was only a few seconds ... maybe since he stumbled, but it may as well have been a minute, or ten minutes. That's how long it felt.

"OK." Farther Carmine said. "There is something you should know about me." He stepped off the podium and crossed the altar. He stood in line with the first row so he would not look at Robert. "I tend get off script sometimes. Call it inspiration from God, or the Holy Spirit, but I will sometimes get different words to say than what are written down for the sermon.

"Like right now.

"So let me ask each and every one of you. Did you ever stop and ask yourself why God made you and place you here? Why now at this time, in this place in the middle of the State instead of Pittsburgh or New York or Miami? Why not China or Brazil?

"That is because God has a purpose for each and every one of us wherever we are. We have a talent and a gift that he wants us to use to the best of our ability. I want you to take that home and think about your lives today."

The service ended soon afterward and the congregation thanked him for the wonderful thought provoking sermon. One straggler stayed behind. When everyone left, he walked up to Father Carmine.

"That was beautiful. It was just like some of the conversations we had back in college."

"What are you doing here?"

"Going to church. What else?"

"I mean, what are you doing HERE, at this parish?"

"It's the closest one to where I live and work. I'm a nurse at the hospital."

"Robert. You can't be here. It's over. Now please go before

someone sees us."

"They'll see a new person talking to the new priest. Besides, you know how I feel about you."

"Robert. I took a vow. I cannot do this."

"I could be an asset to the Church."

"No."

"All right."

The next week Father Carmine agonized over his ex-lover being in town and coming to his church. He had broken off the relationship when he entered the seminary and took the vows. He thought about the repercussions if word got out about a gay relationship he was in.

He was preoccupied with these thoughts all week and it showed when Father Mark came back from the hospital. During play rehearsal, he missed lines and missed his cues as his mind drifted to Robert. Somehow, he had to end this.

On Saturday, Father Carmine sat in the confessional box. He heard several people confess their sins of coveting their neighbor's new television and car but nothing out of the ordinary. One older woman confessed that she did nothing wrong but came to confession weekly because it was good for her soul and she always did so.

The door slid open.

"I have a confession to make Father."

Robert immediately recognized Robert's voice. "Yes. Go on."

"I deeply care for another person. But, if I let my feelings be known, it may jeopardize his future. What should I do?"

Father Carmine thought for a moment. He did not expect this from Robert.

"Is you friend in another relationship?"

"You could say that. He's also a public figure."

"If you openly let your feelings known and others found out, would it do harm to him, either personally or professionally?"

"Yes. I think it would."

"And you say you care for this person?'

"Very much."

"If you care for this person, why would you want to do something that would harm him?"

There was silence on the end.

"What is my penance Father?"

"I leave that up to you."

Father Carmine never saw Robert again.

What A Surprise
Bill McKinley
(854 words)

Father DeBlasio was on a five-mile run around the lake. He couldn't wait to perform his first mass at Holy Angels Church, in two days.

"Hey, Tony," yelled the overweight gentleman he had just passed.

The priest stopped and turned. It was his old high school buddy.

"Hi, Antonio. How are ya? What's it been—thirty years? I just heard about your promotion," the man said, offering a congratulatory handshake.

"Thanks; news sure travels fast in this little town."

"Aw, don't put our little town down. It sure treated us swell. The old neighborhood hasn't changed much. Anyway, old Father Celestino made the announcement during his sermon a coupla weeks ago. He surprised everybody when he said in that Italian accent of his, 'I have a some a gooda news.' Then, he went on ta say a former student from the school was returnin' in two weeks as assistant pastor. Are ya happy ta be comin' back ta your old stompin' grounds?"

"Yes, Carmen, I'm very excited. I've spent the first fifteen years of my priesthood in the big city amidst all the crime and poverty. Although I'll miss helping those lost souls, it will be nice to be able to slow down and offer the parish faithful a one-to-one, hands-on approach to religion, if you know what I mean."

"I do, I do. Man, we're gettin' old; do ya believe we're gonna hit forty-five next year? Unreal!"

"It is very hard to fathom, my friend."

"Say, my aunt's nosy neighbor, Concetta Cedolia, ya know—the old maid that got arrested for stealin' candles right outta the church vestibule and sellin' em in that candy store she use ta own—well, she told my two aunts that she heard from Marcella Basilio—she's the old maid that books numbers over on Cowshit Lane—that your former lover, Maria DeLuca, is a member of your congregation. These old hens don't even attend Holy Angels; they all go ta St. Anastasia's, 'cause they say Father Celestino keeps preachin' about money all the time. I ain't never seen her myself—Maria, that is, probly 'cause I go ta 7 o'clock mass. That's too early for most folks."

"I have to go, Carmine. Hope to see you in church," the shocked cleric replied.

That Sunday, when Father DeBlasio was delivering his homily, he saw *her*. Those eyes . . . as brown as the chocolate drops he used to give her in grade school from CC's Candy Store.

At the conclusion of the service, he sat in his office, reminiscing, and wondering how he would react when he ran into her—which was inevitable.

Antonio recalled the high school romance and college years together; their junior year when they made love for the first time and stared for an eternity into one another's eyes—her into his Paul Newman baby blues, and him into her cocoa-colored, come hither allurements.

Then, came his army draft notice, only two months after their college graduation, while they were planning the wedding for the following spring. Maria promised to wait for her beloved Tony.

After about a year, he wondered why her replies to his letters were not as brisk. Unexpectedly, one month before his two-year discharge, he received the infamous 'Dear John' letter, advising him that she had "accidently" fallen in love with his best friend, Luigi, and they were getting married the following Valentine's Day.

Devastated, he entered the seminary, and after many years of studying Theology and Sacred Scripture, he was ordained. Nonetheless, he had never stopped thinking of her.

Sitting there, he now had doubts about his religious avocation. Was he impetuous? Did he become a priest "on the rebound" or out of spite?

Less than an hour ago, why did his heart drop at a mere glimpse of her, the way one feels at the sight of a police car's blinking lights in the rear-view mirror?

His introspection was abruptly halted by the loud voice of Father Celestino.

"Father DeBlasio, a where have you a been? Aren't you a joining us in the baseament for the breakfast social? You a said you were. The parishioners want a to a meet you. You have only one a chance to make a good first impression, you know?"

"Uh, oh, yes . . . Father, I . . . I was just meditating."

"There's a plenty a time for a that. Come a tend a to your flock."

"Yes, Father, I will be right down."

Antonio descended the stairs, praying that he would not see her.

He entered the spacious room. A young girl shoved a cup of black coffee in front of him.

"Hello Father, my name's Angelina. Would you like cream and sugar, Father?" the cute thing asked, nervously.

"No, thank you. This is fine, Angelina," he replied, pleasantly.

Approaching from behind, Father Celestino startled him again.

"Father DeBlasio, follow a me. There's a someone I a want you to a meet. She a said she's a someone from a your a distant past. Her a name is Ma . . ."

"Hi, Tony. I'm Sister Maria DeLuca."

ABOUT THE AUTHORS

Kerry E.B. Black has long loved words and entices them to create tales both fanciful and true. Hailing from a small suburb situated along a fog-enshrouded river outside of a City of Steel and Bridges, Kerry incorporates Yankee sensibilities and a strong work ethic into every project. She recently became a first reader for *Postcard Poetry and Prose.* Some of her works have crept into anthologies.

She is a proud participant of the www.OneYearofLetters.com project. Kerry writes for www.GamesOmniverse.com and www.Halloweenforevermore.com. She welcomes you to follow her on social media. Twitter @BlackKerryblick, https://kerrylizblack.wordpress.com, and http://www.facebook.com/authorKerryE.B.Black.

Writer, editor, and voice-over talent, **Hana Haatainen-Caye** is the author of *Vinegar Fridays*, as well as over 100 children's books for iStorybooks. Multi-published in the *Chicken Soup for the Soul* anthologies, she is a teacher and coach who is passionate about helping other writers reach their publishing goals. You can follow her on her award-winning blog, Green Grandma www.greengrandma.org or visit her website www.wordsinyourmouth.com.

Deebella (Dolores R.) **Clark** has long loved to read, write and draw. After spending most of her working years in the business world she decided to take some writing classes and pursue that avenue that she loved. By chance she started going to the Springdale Library and began volunteering which later turned into a part time position which she loves. Being a mother of four boys and seven grandchildren she finds many sources of ideas. She thought about retiring, but why would anyone leave the library where all things are possible through reading.
(February 4, 1943 to December 26, 2016)

Estie L. Drum is a graduate of Robert Morris University with a B.S.B.A in Information Systems. Estie enjoys writing as a hobby and finds it therapeutic. A few of her short articles were published in the local news papers, the first when she was in Junior High School. She also conducted an interview and wrote a piece on a summer program for the local church when she worked for The New Pittsburgh Courier. The first book that influenced her, giving her a love of books and storytelling was A Tree Grows in Brooklyn. Estie and her husband, Carl, have been married for 42 years. They have five grown children and seven grandchildren. She has passed the love of story creation, or, as she puts it "making pictures in her head" on to her son Jason, who has picked up the "bug." Estie looks forward to retirement in a few years so she can devote more time to her creations.

Louise Eckman recently retired from a career in Educational Psychology. She consulted with schools and individuals regarding difficulties with reading and/or learning. Since retiring, she has pursued my love of the arts – literature, writing, and music. As a wife, parent and grandparent, she has plenty to write about. She also plays the flute in local music groups.

Susanna Fussenegger is an educator, counselor and a naturalized American citizen since 1972. She is an avid reader. Since childhood she has always known that people enjoyed listening to her stories and hopes to leave one special tale behind for her grandchildren or anyone who cares to read it.

RF Gamgee is the chosen name for a Pittsburgh nerd currently in school for a Master's in Library Science. She's a proud Gryffindor and friend to all dogs.

Dana Colecchia Getz is a writer, teacher and accidental entrepreneur. She lives in Pittsburgh with her husband and two daughters. Spring is her favorite season.

Vicki McCoy Grey, of Springdale, PA, has a B.S.Ed. in Spanish from Clarion State College and an MFA-NFW from Chatham University, both in Pennsylvania. Newly retired, she spends a lot of time writing short stories and experimenting with different styles of writing. She enjoys participating in writing groups to help spark her creative side. She has received several awards for her writing. She enjoyed attending a writing retreat where authors 'became' their character. Ms. Grey has one daughter, who owns Grey Editing in Philadelphia and a six-year granddaughter who likes to write stories and illustrate them. At some point, she plans to work on a book.

Lorelei Hayden is a short story writer, YA novelist and American History teacher from Pittsburgh, PA.

John (J.J.) Hardic is a 1978 graduate of Gannon University where he studied biology and writing. He ascribed to theory of having a backup plan and while writing and perfecting his craft worked in the health care system for over thirty years. John enjoys science fiction/ fantasy and stories which challenge the reader to think. He is influenced by the *Twilight Zone*, the writings of Albert Camus, and enjoys the Dune novels by Frank Herbert. He is an avid Pittsburgh sports fan and brags about being at Three Rivers Stadium for Franco Harris's Immaculate Reception which he did not see. John lives in a Pittsburgh suburb with his wife and four cats.

Always up for a prompt challenge, **Bill Kemp** enjoys writing flash fiction. The novel he completed last year, ***The Exodus of Henry Defazio***, grew out of a short story about a computer nerd who opens his email to discover that his wife is leaving him. Bill also writes nonfiction and has published nine books for church leaders and coauthored a guide for the terminally ill, entitled *Going Home*. His current project is a series of three historical fiction novels set in first century Israel — series title: ***Bethany's People***. He also dabbles in poetry, playwriting, photography, and blogs twice a week at www.billkemp.info.

Dana Kerkentzes is a graduate of Westminster College in New Wilmington, Pennsylvania. Her short stories "Annabel" and "The Christmas Horse" were published in *SCRAWL Literary Magazine,* and her 10-minute play *Cassiopeia* was produced as part of Alpha Psi Omega's One-Act Festival. Dana currently lives and works in the Greater Pittsburgh area with her dog named Kat. When she isn't writing, Dana can usually be found riding her Quarter Horse mare, Pretzel.

Virginia McBurney lives back home in Western Pennsylvania with her retired pastor-husband, Ken. She has done drawing from childhood, but began writing after moving to his first job in Portland, Oregon. Phone calls were too expensive, so communication was a weekly letter about church, her nursing job, and eventually their children's funny words and activities. Ginnie wrote and illustrated a family memoir book, including point-of-view humor stories and poems of pets and things from nature, and also a children's book of Bible quizzes, puzzles, and pictures to color. Gardening, praying, and teaching children drawing uses strength and talent that God gives.

Following retirement, as a benefits administrator for a large corporation, **Bill McKinley** took up writing strictly for pleasure. For almost eight years, he has been a member of *Writers at Work*, a small group of local writers, specializing in fiction. From 2010 through 2015, the Pittsburgh Post-Gazette published 11 of his stories. Bill wrote his childhood memoir, *Memories of a Fatherless, Only Child on Pittsburgh's North Side,* about his growing up in poverty in the 1950's. He self-published the 400-page book in 2011. He also self-published a short mystery novel in 2013 that he wrote for his wife, Sandy. It's entitled, *The Girl with the Storybook Eyes*, with settings in Ireland and Florida.

Jenifer McNamara lives near Pittsburgh with her family and their dog Duke, who enjoys listening to her stories. She graduated from Bradford Business School in Pittsburgh, PA. She has attended several writing conferences, taken courses, and won a few medals for her writing.

Debra Sanchez leads and attends various writing groups in the Pittsburgh area and also hosts writing retreats. Her writing has won awards at writers conferences in various genres, including children's stories, poetry, fantasy, fiction, and creative nonfiction. Several of her plays and monologues have been produced and published. Other works have been published in literary magazines, newspapers, and anthologies. ***Pages: A Library Play*** was recently translated and published in Spanish as ***Páginas: Un Cuento de Bibliotecas***. For more information, visit her webpage:
www.DebraRSanchez.com , follow her on
Facebook: @DebraRSanchez and Twitter: @DebraRSanchez

Isabella Sanchez wrote the story "Hello Kitty Meets The Joker" at age 9. She lives a few minutes from Minneapolis, MN with her parents and younger brother. When she isn't writing stories, she loves to spend time reading and making videos. She enjoys camping, and skiing and plays basketball, soccer, and volleyball.

Megan Vance discovered her love of writing in midlife. She likes to write non-fiction, children's, poetry and magazine articles and some were published in different magazines and in the Pittsburgh Post- Gazette. Her first book, a devotional called ***Sure Mercies: Hope for the Suffering***, was published by 4RV Publishing in the fall of 2015. When not writing she loves spending time with her grandsons, sewing, quilting, or reading. She is married to Kevin and is the mother of three adult children.

INDEX by AUTHOR

ABOUT THE EDITOR

Debra R. Sanchez has moved over thirty times... so far. She and her husband have three adult children, four grandchildren, as well as a cat and a dog. She leads and attends various writing groups in the Pittsburgh area and also hosts writing retreats. Her writing has won awards at writers conferences in various genres, including children's stories, poetry, fantasy, fiction, and creative nonfiction. Several of her plays and monologues have been produced and published. Her work has been published in literary magazines, local newspapers, and anthologies.

For more information, visit her webpage:

www.DebraRSanchez.com

Follow her on Facebook: @DebraRSanchez

and Twitter: @DebraRSanchez

www.ingramcontent.com/pod-product-compliance
Lightning Source LLC
Chambersburg PA
CBHW021045090426
42738CB00006B/192